DATE DUE

ISSUES THAT CONCERN YOU

Disaster Relief

Hayley Mitchell Haugen, *Book Editor*
with Bruce Elkins, Katie Fugett, Kacy Lovelace,
Olivia Picklesimer, and Emily Mays

GREENHAVEN PRESS
A part of Gale, Cengage Learning

GALE
CENGAGE Learning

Detroit • New York • San Francisco • New Haven, Conn • Waterville, Maine • London

Christine Nasso, *Publisher*
Elizabeth Des Chenes, *Managing Editor*

For more information, contact:
Greenhaven Press
27500 Drake Rd.
Farmington Hills, MI 48331-3535
Or you can visit our Internet site at gale.cengage.com

For product information and technology assistance, contact us at

Gale Customer Support, 1-800-877-4253
For permission to use material from this text or product, submit all requests online at www.cengage.com/permissions

Further permissions questions can be emailed to permissionrequest@cengage.com

Articles in Greenhaven Press anthologies are often edited for length to meet page requirements. In addition, original titles of these works are changed to clearly present the main thesis and to explicitly indicate the author's opinion. Every effort is made to ensure that Greenhaven Press accurately reflects the original intent of the authors. Every effort has been made to trace the owners of copyrighted material.

This book was researched, written, and edited collaboratively with the book editor by the following: Bruce Elkins, Katie Fugett, Kacy Lovelace, Olivia Picklesimer, and Emily Mays.

Cover image: Chris Graythen/Getty Images

LIBRARY OF CONGRESS CATALOGING-IN-PUBLICATION DATA

Disaster relief / Hayley Mitchell Haugen, book editor.
    p. cm. -- (Issues that concern you)
 Includes bibliographical references and index.
 ISBN 978-0-7377-4494-1 (hardcover)
 1. Disaster relief--United States--Juvenile literature. 2. United States. Federal
Emergency Management Agency--Juvenile literature. [1. Emergency management--
United States--Juvenile literature.] I. Haugen, Hayley Mitchell, 1968-
 HV555.U6D582 2009
 363.34'80973--dc22
                                                                 2009018272

Printed in the United States of America
1 2 3 4 5 6 7 13 12 11 10 09

CONTENTS

Hurricane Katrina came violently ashore along the Gulf Coast of the United States on August 29, 2005. The 125-mile-per-hour winds and the enormous waves of the category three storm—one of the biggest in the United States in the past one hundred years—did their greatest damage as they pounded the coast of Louisiana, breaking the levee system built to protect the citizens of New Orleans and surrounding areas. As a result of the faulty levee system, 80 percent of New Orleans flooded, causing billions of dollars in structural damage. Thousands of people in the coastal regions of Louisiana and Mississippi lost their homes and businesses in the flooding, and many others lost their lives. Over eighteen hundred people died as a result of the hurricane and subsequent flooding. According to the Earth Institute at Columbia University, over nine hundred of these people were from New Orleans alone.

In times of such a catastrophic disaster as Hurricane Katrina, American citizens have come to expect swift and effective disaster relief from their government. With the passage of the Disaster Relief Act of 1974, the American president has the power to declare a state of emergency during natural disasters. This declaration carries with it the official financial and tactical approval for federal agencies to provide disaster relief to affected areas. This aid may include evacuating citizens from dangerous environments; providing food, water, shelter, and medical attention; and assisting with the permanent relocation of affected people, if necessary. The people of New Orleans had no reason to suspect that this traditional form of aid would not be quickly forthcoming from government officials, yet precisely because they did *not* receive the level of aid they were expecting, the Katrina disaster has become the most controversial hurricane in American history.

Former president George W. Bush has been criticized for not making his disaster declaration for a large enough area at the onset of the storm. The Federal Emergency Management

The Disaster Relief Act of 1974 gave the president the power to declare a state of emergency to free up federal aid in times of catastrophic disaster, such as Hurricane Katrina.

Agency (FEMA) has likewise come under attack by many people who believe that mismanagement of the organization delayed relief efforts, especially for some thirty thousand people stranded in New Orleans after the storm. Because many of Hurricane Katrina's victims were African Americans, others claim that the delayed aid was more a case of racial discrimination than mismanagement.

While many people do praise the government and FEMA for the lives that *were* saved during the Katrina disaster and for the homeless families that have since received federal assistance with housing, many other Americans' faith in U.S. disaster relief has shattered. Some people believe that the government should not be in charge of disaster relief at all or that government should at least partner more effectively with the private sector during times of crisis. Indeed, American companies such as Wal-Mart and Home Depot have already proven that they are both willing and capable of assisting with disaster relief efforts.

In a September 6, 2005, article, NewsMax.com journalists reported on Wal-Mart's humanitarian role during Hurricane Katrina for their "Story Behind the Story" column. The company, they said, was being commended for its relief efforts. Wal-Mart Stores, Inc., which, by the way, has its own high-tech hurricane tracking and command centers, bolstered the supplies in its Gulf Coast stores before Hurricane Katrina came ashore. Impressed by Wal-Mart's response, Burr Flickinger III, the managing director for Strategic Resource Group in New York, told the Associated Press, "Unlike local, state and the federal government, which didn't react until days after the hurricane hit, Wal-Mart was at work around the clock before Katrina even hit land to have the stores fully stocked with full pallet positions of water, flashlights, batteries, canned soup, canned meat." The additional merchandise helped residents prepare for the storm in advance of the disaster. In addition to helping storm-area residents help themselves, Wal-Mart Stores, Inc., donated millions of dollars in cash and goods to relief efforts once Katrina hit land. These donations included more than one hundred trailer loads of goods to emergency relief organizations, services, and shelters.

The corporation later pledged $15 million to the building of a relief plan to handle future disasters, sponsored by former presidents George H.W. Bush and Bill Clinton. While Flickinger also praised the relief effort contributions of other well-known corporate giants, such as Home Depot Inc., Lowe's, and Walgreen Co., in his view, Wal-Mart deserves special recognition for "serv[ing] the city far better than any private or public institution."

Questions about the extent to which the American government should remain in charge of disaster relief, versus allowing private companies such as Wal-Mart to play a larger role, make up just a small percentage of America's critical conversation about disaster relief. The authors in this anthology help readers explore the controversial aspects of disaster relief more thoroughly. In addition to discussions about the operation of FEMA and other relief organizations, the articles' argumentative topics examine disaster relief spending and the process of overseeing these institutions. Other articles focus on the human toll in the wake of natural disasters, such as the many thousands of people left homeless after Hurricane Katrina, or the plight of undocumented workers during the wildfire season in California. The collection's contributors also present opinions on saving pets during disaster relief efforts, the value of volunteerism during disasters, and much more.

Finally, this text includes a selective bibliography and a list of organizations to contact for additional information to help readers further engage with the topic. The appendix titled "What You Should Know About Disaster Relief" provides current facts about disaster relief. The appendix "What You Should Do About Disaster Relief" suggests tips to young readers for preparing for various kinds of natural disasters and remaining safe should a disaster occur in their area. With all of these features, *Issues That Concern You: Disaster Relief* provides an excellent resource during a time when news-savvy readers may be concerned about the effect of natural disasters on people worldwide.

ONE

An Effective Disaster Relief System Is Crucial

Gilbert Burnham

> Gilbert Burnham is professor of international health at the Johns Hopkins Bloomberg School of Public Health and codirector of the Johns Hopkins Center for Refugee and Disaster Response. In this viewpoint Burnham argues that failures in national disaster management complicate relief efforts and increase the severity of disasters. Burnham believes that even a very primitive response system would be effective enough to save property and lives. He argues in favor of a disaster relief fund that would allow for more preparedness. He says that a disaster relief fund would also help alleviate the financial burden placed on organizations such as the American Red Cross.

[L ate 2004–early 2006 has] seen major disasters in Asia, Africa, and the Americas. Hundreds of thousands of people have died and millions have had their lives changed forever. Some attention has focused on a possible increase in the frequency of natural and man-made hazards that are responsible for these disasters. However, the right place for our attention is on the increasing vulnerabilities related to geography and livelihood. As new disasters occur in 2006, we cannot lose sight of what we should have learned from the disasters of 2004 and 2005. Serious

Gilbert Burnham, "Preventing Disaster: Realizing Vulnerabilities and Looking Forward," *Harvard International Review*, Spring 2006. Reproduced by permission.

thinking on these lessons can protect the lives of those who continue to live in circumstances particularly vulnerable to disaster. These are issues we cannot further delay addressing.

How the world responded to the tragedy of the December 26 [2004] tsunami will continue to be examined in detail through expert panels, workshops, and reports. The same will be true for Hurricane Katrina and the Kashmir earthquake. Less attention will be paid to the planning and preparation that could have mitigated these disasters. Predictably, only some passing mention will be made about the lack of community disaster management capacity or the manifest failure to reduce the obvious vulnerabilities that resulted in widespread loss of life and property.

Red Cross volunteers coordinate Katrina relief efforts. For a variety of reasons, the organization fell short in its relief effort.

The Need for an Effective Response System

At the heart of these disasters was the failure to develop effective national disaster management capacity—the capacity to plan and prepare for response, to coordinate assistance, to develop policies on reconstruction, and to confront the vulnerabilities of the population.

Development of a national disaster response system stretches from policy formation in central government to community preparedness. It is a plodding and unexciting process that requires updated legislation and emergency operations plans at many levels and in many sectors. A variety of often disparate stakeholders must plan together, competing goals and highly variable capacities must be reconciled, training programs must be required, and capacities must be repeatedly tested. These initiatives need not be expensive to be effective, as demonstrated by cyclone response programs in Bangladesh and hurricane preparedness efforts in the Caribbean states. They require perseverance and unified focus by a capable team as well as consistent political support. External organizations also play an important role in helping make this happen.

The popular image of disasters comes from pictures on television of the desperate homeowner, the harried relief worker, and the various logos of relief organizations. Little credit is given to the long and unflagging support provided by the International Federation of Red Cross and Red Crescent Societies, the consistent efforts of the Pan American Health Organization, or the work of the United Nations Development Programme (UNDP) in helping countries build their disaster management capacities in quiet and undramatic ways.

There have been no headline-grabbing presidential initiatives for disaster preparedness, no Millennium Goals for disaster management. The UN International Decade for Natural Disaster Reduction quietly closed its doors in 2000 and its successor, the International Strategy for Disaster Reduction, is not making big waves. Promising major disaster relief initiatives or sending prominent public officials, such as former presidents and prime ministers, could give disaster preparedness a higher media profile.

An all-out effort on the part of prosperous nations to strengthen disaster management capacity in less developed countries is the only way to create long-term stability and reduce human and economic losses worldwide.

A Disaster Response Fund Is Necessary

Responding to specific disasters by providing hand-to-mouth help is not the best way to help countries suffering from the effects of a natural disaster. Creating a standing fund to draw from to meet disaster needs immediately, sidestepping the present flash appeal process, could speed relief and make for more effective intervention. Some disasters are more photogenic and emotion-laden than others, eliciting more funds. But even when developed countries pledge funds for a disaster, these pledges may not be fully honored. Proposals from UN agencies for a large general disaster response fund have been rejected by the United States and other prospective donors, but the idea must be revisited. Ways to make disaster relief funds more quickly available must be explored.

In most locations, tsunami disaster assistance was oversubscribed, leaving some agencies with funds they could not easily expend in a sound manner. Doctors Without Borders closed its appeal for tsunami relief when it became evident that there would be problems spending everything received, an ethical response. Other agencies did not always respect the same principles.

For a variety of reasons, donations for those affected by Hurricane Katrina fell short. The American Red Cross had to borrow money for disaster relief, hoping that future donations would cover the debt. The US government seems to be backing away from its initial funding promises or at least looking for ways to pay for relief and reconstruction by reducing benefits for marginal groups. For the impoverished of New Orleans, Congress may be delivering a second Katrina.

Disasters, as portrayed by the media, often drive individuals and donor nations to fund relief activities. Tsunami relief was very generous, but aid for the recent food crises in Southern Africa was a pittance compared to what was needed. It has been the reflex response of many humanitarians to blame the media for

Cartoon by Ed Fischer, www.CartoonStock.com.

publicizing some emergencies but not others, skewing donations. However, the media are newshounds, not humanitarians; some disasters generate more appealing stories than others. The relief community itself carries some of the blame for publicizing crises in a fund-raising mode rather than a more analytical mode. The careful work on mortality in the Eastern Congo by the International Rescue Committee and the work of CARE in assessing the deterioration of nutritional status among the Palestinians in Gaza and the West Bank are encouraging examples. Another organization, the International Crisis Group, offers a badly needed political analysis capacity that can help agencies understand how to provide effective assistance in complex situations.

Over the past decade the technical response to disasters has improved substantially, often through careful evaluation of refugee programs. Important milestones in improving response have been the creation of the Sphere Project technical standards for disaster response and the Code of Conduct for humanitarian response. Drug policies for emergencies have been created by the World Health Organization, and academic courses for disaster management and disaster research have been developed.

TWO

The Government Should Not Be in Charge of Disaster Relief

Matt Ryan

Matt Ryan is an adjunct fellow with the Independent Institute in Oakland, California, and holds a master's degree in economics from San Jose State University. Ryan argues in this viewpoint that disaster relief is used as a means to further political aims and pass political agendas. Ryan contends that states whose congressional representatives are involved in Federal Emergency Management Agency (FEMA) oversight receive more disaster declarations from the president and therefore receive more financial aid for disaster relief. Ryan also believes that the federal government, through FEMA, should not be in charge of disaster relief or in charge of disaster relief security in the United States because it does not perform the job adequately.

In times of natural disaster, people often look to government for solutions. Sadly, it seems that politicians use disasters to further their political careers.

Matt Ryan, "Take the Politics Out of Disaster Relief," *Independent Institute*, September 30, 2005. Reproduced by permission of The Independent Institute, 100 Swan Way, Oakland, CA 94021-1428 USA. www.independent.org.

A prophetic article published in *Economic Inquiry* two years ago, by Thomas Garrett of the Federal Reserve Bank of St. Louis and Russell Sobel of West Virginia University, shows how alarmingly political disaster relief really is. Garrett and Sobel found that from 1991 to 1999 states that were more politically important to the president had a higher rate of natural-disaster declarations. Further, the average number of disasters declared in election years was 66 percent higher than the number in non-election years, yet there is little reason to believe that bad weather mimics political cycles.

They also find that states that had congressional representation on [Federal Emergency Management Agency] (FEMA) oversight

Salvation Army volunteers man a food distribution center for Katrina victims. The author argues that organizations like the Salvation Army are better equipped for natural disaster relief than the government.

committees received higher disaster expenditures. Their model estimates that for each House member on an oversight committee, the Representative's home state receives $31 million in excess disaster expenditures. They estimate that nearly half of all disaster relief from 1991 to 1999 was devoted to furthering political goals.

Economist Alan Krueger noted in a [2005] *New York Times* article that President [George W.] Bush declared 61 major disasters in election-year 2004, an increase of 10 disasters over 2003. In battleground states where the election was decided by five percentage points or less, the number of major disasters increased to 17 in 2004 from 8 in 2003—90 percent of the election-year rise.

Disasters Are Used to Further Political Agendas

Disaster declarations provide a unique opportunity for government officials to push pork to constituents without the usual scrutiny. While especially ill-conceived federal spending measures are often reported in the media, disaster relief spending is questioned rarely. For example, last December [2004,] Ohio was declared a disaster area after getting only two feet of snow, yet few questioned the decision.

Federally funded disaster relief is not used efficiently because officials don't face the same discipline that people face in private markets. The journey of an ice truck providing Katrina relief illustrates FEMA's inability to coordinate and its blindness to cost effectiveness. After leaving Wisconsin and arriving in Louisiana, the truck was sent to Georgia but then rerouted to South Carolina. After ending up in Maryland, the truck's ice sat stationary for days, while costing taxpayers money and leaving those in need of relief with fewer supplies.

FEMA's blindness to cost has become even more apparent with the awarding of rebuilding contracts to government favorites, such as Halliburton and Bechtel, without a competitive bidding process. Those that issue the contracts cite the need for expediency, and claim that no-bid contracts went to "proven" contractors able to assist quickly in reconstruction. Unfortunately, the only thing that no-bid government contracting has "proven" is that it accomplishes wasteful spending and inflated prices.

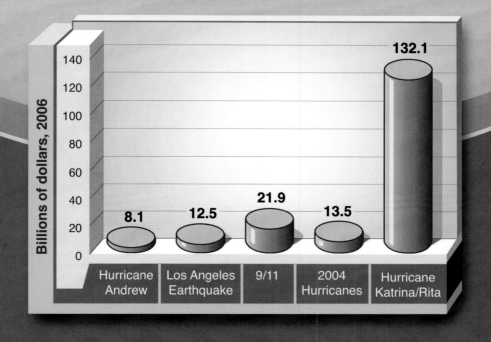

The Cost of Government Response to Domestic Emergencies

Billions of dollars, 2006

Hurricane Andrew	Los Angeles Earthquake	9/11	2004 Hurricanes	Hurricane Katrina/Rita
8.1	12.5	21.9	13.5	132.1

Taken from: Senate Budget Committee Majority Staff, June 4, 2007.

Companies in the private sector have profits and losses to ensure that goods are being allocated efficiently; the public sector has no such information by which to make economically sound decisions. When prices rise after a disaster companies are given the information and incentive to send in more of the needed goods. FEMA instead operates on the basis of how its actions impact the political careers of those who appoint its directors and allocate its budget.

FEMA Should Be Removed from the Equation

To better deal with disasters, FEMA's role should be reduced as much as possible—ideally eliminated—and private organizations should be encouraged to take over relief duties. President Bush has recently suggested that the Pentagon should play a larger role in disaster relief, but it hardly seems fit for government to play a larger role in disaster relief when it currently performs so poorly.

The performance of the Salvation Army and Red Cross illustrate how the private sector can provide effective, pointed disaster relief in an efficient manner. Unlike FEMA, the Salvation Army is forced to be effective in its distribution of aid because the vitality of the Salvation Army comes from voluntary donations. If it doesn't do its job well, donors will send their donations elsewhere. FEMA faces no such constraint because it gets its money through the political system. It should be no surprise that politics motivates its decisions.

FEMA is also given the responsibility of providing security. Rioting and mob-like activity hampered initial relief efforts in New Orleans, and an effective security force would have expedited relief efforts. Unfortunately, FEMA was busy stopping another movement—that of private charities into the disaster area. FEMA forced the Salvation Army and Red Cross to remain out of New Orleans during the first days immediately following Katrina's wrath. Perhaps security would be better handled by others, as well.

The *Economist* magazine called the Katrina disaster the "Shaming of America," but they got it wrong. The outpouring of private charity has been remarkable and Americans should be proud. What has been shameful is our government's catastrophic handling of disaster relief.

THREE

Americans Need a Better Understanding of FEMA

Daniel J. Kaniewski

> Daniel J. Kaniewski is senior director for response policy at the White House and formerly special assistant to the president for homeland security. He defends the Federal Emergency Management Agency (FEMA) by explaining in this viewpoint how the agency works. He believes that the reason why the public has such a bad opinion of FEMA is due mostly to misunderstandings of FEMA's actual role in disaster relief. Kaniewski explains that FEMA is no more than a coordinator of the different agencies and resources that the government has available to them. He feels that FEMA is better prepared for the next disaster, and he gives credit for the many improvements to the new management, Dave Paulison and Harvey Johnson.

When Hurricane Gustav approached Louisiana, I was asked a question familiar during my time in the post-Katrina White House. Is [the Federal Emergency Management Agency] (FEMA) ready? For the past three years, I have said that the real question we should be asking ourselves is: Are we ready? FEMA is an easy target; its four-letter acronym is often used as shorthand to convey all of Katrina's failures. But FEMA is

Reasons People Would Not Evacuate During Hurricane Gustav

1. Previous false alarms about previous hurricanes.

2. The fear that they would not be able to get back to their homes to fend off looters.

3. Refusing to deal with the chaos and gridlock of the evacuation.

4. Many did not have the money to fill up their gas tanks.

5. Trying to make a show of bravery in the face of the storm.

Taken from: Ben Casselman and Ana Campoy, "Many Weren't Scared Enough to Flee," *The Wall Street Journal*, September 15, 2008. http://online.wsj.com.

just one piece of the preparedness puzzle. The organization is relatively new by historical standards, having been created as an independent agency in 1979. Before that time, disaster-response activities were scattered amongst some 100 federal agencies. In 2003, FEMA was brought under the Department of Homeland Security. Regardless of the agency's placement in the federal bureaucracy, there are fundamental misunderstandings of FEMA's role and mission which drive false expectations by the public.

The Way FEMA Works, Exactly

The federal government rarely becomes actively involved in responding to incidents. For example, if you are not feeling well, you may choose to visit the doctor's office. If you are very sick, and do not have transportation, you may dial 911. But certainly you would not expect an ambulance emblazoned with FEMA to show up at your doorstep. This is clearly a responsibility of the local government. The story becomes a more complicated one when state and local resources are overwhelmed and there are not enough ambulances, for example, to evacuate all those who require medical transport. When Gustav came ashore [in 2008], FEMA had pre-positioned hundreds of ambulances near the projected impact area. But even so, these ambulances were not FEMA ambulances either. They were ambulances under contract from private companies to be available to FEMA, so that they could be provided to supplement state and local resources.

So even if state and local officials request the federal government's help, there are no FEMA ambulances, helicopters, and buses. FEMA coordinates amongst all levels of government, contracts with the private sector, and leverages personnel and resources from the federal government. Sometimes this system works well, as is the case with the greatly strengthened relationship between FEMA and the Department of Defense; other times not, such as when Louisiana's pre-established contract for buses fell through as Gustav approached, forcing the state and FEMA to quickly consider other options. Thus, FEMA is only as strong as its weakest link, with FEMA failing if a contractor, or a local, state or federal agency, stumbles.

Critics could argue that the agency has simply not been tested the way Katrina stressed the organization, and thus we do not know how well prepared FEMA is to deal with the next disaster. While it is true we have had two light hurricane seasons, there have been many other disasters such as the widespread Midwest flooding, severe California wildfires and the record tornado season that would have highlighted any significant FEMA shortcomings.

FEMA Transformed Under New Leadership

I witnessed the transformation of the organization since Katrina and attribute much to the vision (and ambition) of its capable leadership. Dave Paulison, a respected former fire chief and emergency manager, along with his deputy Harvey Johnson, a retired Coast Guard admiral, took the helm of an organization that was broken and demoralized. They sought jobs nobody wanted and made it their mission to succeed. They brought innovative thinking about tough problems facing the agency; sought 21st century technology; recruited respected professionals from the emergency management community; and strived to serve their federal, state and local stakeholders. Messrs. Paulison and Johnson even fought tough internal turf battles at DHS [Department of Homeland Security] at the same time they battled public opinion post-Katrina. Today, FEMA is still growing, still innovating, still

The author asserts that Dave Paulison (pictured), the acting director of FEMA, has transformed the organization with innovative thinking so that it is better prepared to effectively manage disaster relief.

learning while it responds to a seemingly endless array of disasters. The American public seems to understand the federal government is better prepared today than it was at Katrina, and much of that credit is due to FEMA's improvements. Even inside DHS, where there had been a rocky relationship between the agency and its parent organization long before Katrina struck, there is a newfound respect for FEMA.

Now with Hurricane Ike looming in Gulf waters, FEMA readies not just its own organization, but also is unifying the entire federal government for a common purpose—a rarity in Washington. I, for one, am glad this isn't my father's FEMA.

FEMA Needs Better Operations Management

Richard Sylves

> Richard Sylves has researched disaster policies for more than fifteen years. He is an author and professor of political science at the University of Delaware. In this viewpoint Sylves criticizes the Federal Emergency Management Agency (FEMA) for not using the fundamental skills of operations management (OM) to organize for disasters. He claims that even the smallest businesses effectively use OM principles to meet supply and demand needs accordingly. Sylves argues his point for the need of better OM in FEMA by exploring how customer-oriented agencies are able to provide the best services to their clientele.

In the wake of the poor government response to the 2005 Hurricane Katrina disaster, many questions have been asked about why the U.S. Federal Emergency Management Agency (FEMA), along with a host of other federal, state, and local emergency management agencies, performed so ineffectively. What went wrong? What is the future of the agency? How can a recurrence of the Katrina debacle be prevented? This article explores whether FEMA and other disaster management agencies may

Richard Sylves, "FEMA, Katrina, and Operations Research: Better Operations Management Would Have Helped FEMA in Preparedness and Response Work Before Hurricane Katrina and Still Could Now," *The Public Manager*, vol. 37, Spring 2008, pp. 68–71. Copyright © 2008 *The Public Manager*. All rights reserved. Reproduced by permission.

have overlooked the importance of "operations research" and "operations management" (OM) in preparedness and response work before Hurricane Katrina struck in 2005.

Many investigations followed in the aftermath of Hurricane Katrina in late 2005 through 2006. Communications problems were alleged to be a factor. Poor leadership of FEMA was another claim. Failures of intergovernmental relations, particularly between the president and the governor of Louisiana, were also put forward.

The congressional report, *Failure of Initiative,* constantly refers to FEMA's problems in maintaining "situational awareness." Might it be that FEMA, when it needed to function as a "machine bureaucracy" in the interest of accelerated response to public needs created by the Katrina catastrophe, did not employ enough managers with the requisite OM skill sets needed for such circumstances? Might it also be that FEMA officials were not prepared to make predisaster arrangements with private contractors and nonprofit organizations on the basis of sound OM principles?

"Operations managers" possess skills and abilities that could help deliver smoother, faster, and more efficient disaster relief.

The Relief System Is to Blame for Delayed Responses

Once Hurricane Katrina made landfall along the Gulf Coast, FEMA faced a disaster of catastrophic proportions. When the levees in New Orleans collapsed, a second catastrophe compounded the problem. Some allege that FEMA simply was not ready for a disaster of Katrina's complexity and magnitude. [Author] James Miskel argues that FEMA is capable of handling routine disasters but not catastrophic ones. He contends that no national government agency, regardless of state and local help, could be expected to manage a catastrophe, and he sees Katrina as a catastrophe. Confirming or refuting Miskel's claim is difficult because identifying the threshold that separates "routine" from "catastrophic" disasters is problematic.

After Katrina struck, tens of thousands of people were displaced from their homes, a thousand more were dead, and many needed rescue. FEMA found itself in the national spotlight. The agency, working under its new and largely untested National Response Plan (NRP), could not provide enough relief fast enough for all of the people in need. Examples of FEMA bungling were widespread, many recounted in Douglas Brinkley's extraordinary book *The Great Deluge*. Communications between FEMA and state and local authorities were inadequate. A major political "blame game" ensued as news media people and a host of elected government officials sought to identify who was responsible for the slowness and deficiencies in government emergency response.

In mid-September 2005, FEMA Director Michael D. Brown resigned from his position, helping to absorb or deflect considerable blame directed at the [George W.] Bush administration. The reasons for the inadequate intergovernmental response to Hurricane Katrina and its aftermath are many, so laying the blame on one or a handful of government officials is shortsighted. The system by which relief is dispensed in a catastrophic disaster is a major part of the problem.

Operations Management Keeps Businesses Efficient

OM is the part of the business world that focuses on the "process" a firm uses to provide a product or service to the consumer. At its most basic, it is the transformation process that takes raw materials, labor, and capital and turns them into final products or services, adding value for the customer. The goal of OM is to produce a product or a service in the most efficient way.

People like Henry Ford and Eli Whitney conceived and then applied their ideas to a working environment in which efficiency was given primacy. The assembly line and cotton gin are examples of OM thinking. These figures and many others throughout history were simply looking for the cheapest and most efficient way to produce a product.

During Katrina, thousands of people were displaced from their homes and gathered at the New Orleans Superdome for an evacuation that was handicapped by FEMA's poor operations management during the disaster.

Although people like Ford and Whitney were not educated in the field of OM, their approaches were perfectly consistent with it. In the early part of the twentieth century, the field began to flourish. OM is consistent with the scientific management approach, widely popular in public administration and the corporate world from the 1920s to the 1950s. The bureaucratic model associated with scientific management has a host of drawbacks, but operations research and management should not be abandoned. In the mid-1900s many in U.S. universities were drawn to the precision, logic, and functionality of operations research. . . .

FEMA Would Benefit from Adopting Business Principles

FEMA, though a government agency, has much in common with a private business. Both provide services or products, and both face a demand curve that varies. Ironically, FEMA relies on a host of contractors to furnish disaster relief. Many of these firms are themselves for profit private-sector businesses.

A business provides either a product or service to a consumer. In many respects, FEMA provides, either directly or indirectly, services and products to "consumers." Former FEMA Director James Lee Witt used to tout the agency's success in "customer satisfaction." In this vein, FEMA provides disaster relief and funding to people living in areas devastated by disaster, information to disaster victims, a system for requesting certain forms of aid, and in-kind commodities—usually through various contractors and suppliers or through government-stored commodities.

Like a business, the demand for FEMA's services and commodities varies daily. When the president declares a major disaster in a state and its affected counties, the demand for FEMA's services

Cartoon by Ed Fischer, www.CartoonStock.com.

and commodities increases in that locale. Conversely, FEMA does not need to provide as many services or commodities in locales not declared disasters.

From 1953 to 2007, the president declared almost 1,700 disasters, and from 1974 to 2007, almost 300 emergencies. Mapping the location and frequency of such declarations, identifying the type of disaster agent involved, and modeling and projecting the recurrence of many of them are all possible. Susan Cutter's book *American Hazardscapes* and the Public Entity Risk Institute's presidential disaster declaration Web site (developed by the author) provide location information about federally declared disasters in the United States. Although seemingly simplistic, if companies such as Lowe's, Home Depot, and McDonald's can model where customer demand is for their products and configure production, supply, and retail operations accordingly, FEMA could do the same.

Much was made of FedEx and UPS carrier business effectiveness as a model for how FEMA should have operated after Hurricane Katrina. Although the comparison is unfair in many respects, FEMA could benefit from emulating the OM traits of those businesses and others that depend on tightly coupled, highly reliable services. The excuse that disasters are too infrequent to be predicted or anticipated is not wholly valid.

Simply achieving more "situational awareness" by adding more video capacity and network communications to address future Katrina-scale catastrophes is not the total solution to better disaster relief dispensation. It's what disaster managers actually do with the added information that counts. . . .

Operations Management Is Needed for Improvement

All organizations have an inventory of equipment, including the people employed and actual equipment, such as computers, food items, and blankets. Operations managers have acquired skills that allow them to recognize the inventory items, quantities, and locations needed, while seeking to minimize costs. Consider the problem of vaccines needed to address the threat of pandemic disease. The U.S. Department of Homeland Security's NRP states, "Shortages of available supplies of preventive and therapeutic pharmaceuticals and qualified medical personnel to administer available prophylaxis are likely." Problems like these can be solved; personnel with OM backgrounds can address them.

Arguably, OM approaches to disaster management would help FEMA reduce waste and trim the costs of disaster for the national taxpayer. In disaster mitigation programs, such as those involving buyout or relocation decisions, operations managers could assist in decision making, particularly for planners facilitating resettlement.

Operations managers can help FEMA in many other ways, providing leadership, organization, and other skills. Some personnel within FEMA have business backgrounds, and some have experience in OM, but a great many do not. People with OM expertise could help improve FEMA's sorely tested tele-registration system of applicant assistance. They could tutor FEMA contracting officers in acquisition efforts to solicit bids from and make awards to vendors that incorporate OM tenets into these arrangements.

OM is a field FEMA officials should consider in their hiring practices. People with expertise in this field possess skills in leadership, organization, and inventory management. Any evaluation of FEMA's performance in disaster relief, whether in Hurricane Katrina or any other disaster, should gauge its facility in the use of OM principles. This could improve predisaster preparedness and postdisaster response. People with political and generalist backgrounds are still needed in FEMA, but the agency would be wise to recruit more managers with operations research education and experience.

FIVE

The Media Can Keep the Government in Check During Disaster Relief Efforts

Rem Rieder

Rem Rieder is the editor and senior vice president of the *American Journalism Review,* a publication that covers all aspects of print, television, radio, and online media. In this viewpoint Rieder praises American journalists for their coverage of Hurricane Katrina in 2005. Rieder contends that reporters had become timid in the wake of the 9/11 attacks, not wanting to question the government's reaction to the tragedy for fear of seeming un-American. The devastation caused by Hurricane Katrina, however, renewed journalists' commitment to reporting the truth, Rieder says. They put their own lives on the line to report the Katrina story, and they held government officials responsible for bumbling disaster relief efforts during the crisis.

Journalism matters.

We hold that truth to be self-evident. But in recent years the proposition has taken quite a battering.

The litany of woe for the proud but beleaguered profession is painfully familiar. The shrinking audiences. The endless string

Rem Rieder, "Playing Big: The Media's Impressive Coverage of Hurricane Katrina," *American Journalism Review*, vol. 27, October/November 2005, p. 6. Reproduced by permission of *American Journalism Review*.

A reporter interviews a federal relief coordinator about ongoing evacuation efforts in New Orleans.

of plagiarism and fabrication cases. The Wall Street–fueled cutbacks. The post-9/11 timidity. The WMD [weapons of mass destruction] blunder. It was almost enough to make the most starry-eyed optimist embrace the blogosphere's ubiquitous obits for the so-15-minutes-ago mainstream media.

Then Hurricane Katrina decimated the Gulf Coast and the [George W.] Bush administration dithered and stumbled. And the MSM [mainstream media] rose to the occasion.

Television's powerful images brought home the unfathomable horrors of New Orleans. Newspapers provided incisive and comprehensive coverage. Local radio served as a lifeline for a devastated region.

People were starved for information. And journalists, brave, committed journalists, went out and got it for them, often under harrowing conditions.

As [*Washington Post* columnist] Marc Fisher points out . . . suddenly the notion that there is value in having trained professionals on the scene to cover the news didn't seem quite so quaint.

Katrina Journalists Held Government Accountable

That the media performed well is hardly a surprise. Journalists live to cover the big story. Acts of nature—what one writer I know calls "big weather"—have always brought out the best in reporters and news organizations.

But this time there was more to the picture. What was particularly impressive was the fact that journalists were ready, even eager, to hold officialdom accountable, to cut through the gobble-dygook. That's a very welcome development.

For years the Washington press corps took a skeptical approach toward people in power. In fact, there were those who thought the press was too aggressive, too confrontational, too quick to poke holes, too rarely willing to transmit the messages of political leaders.

But after 9/11, much of the media seemed cowed, afraid to press too hard, as if questioning the Bush administration's pronouncements about terrorism was somehow unpatriotic. The overly credulous approach to the notion that Saddam [Hussein] had weapons of mass destruction is a vivid example of the phenomenon, but hardly the only one.

That's not meant to be a blanket indictment. Certainly many news organizations have done a fine job in reporting from [the war in] Iraq, in depicting a situation that often bears little resemblance to the rosy, what-me-worry pronouncements of the war's architects.

With Katrina, the chasm between the platitudes of the clueless government spokesmen and the ugly reality of New Orleans—the devastation, the misery, the Third World–style chaos—was overwhelming.

And journalists from Ted Koppel to Tim Russert to Shepard Smith were simply unwilling to hold back from calling the bumbling bureaucrats on their pitiful delusions.

Journalists Must Report the Truth

And good for them. Because that's the job of journalists—to report the truth. That's not always comfortable. It doesn't always make you the most popular guy in town. But it's the right thing to do. Let's hope Katrina buries forever the notion of false equivalency, the idea that fair and balanced reporting means giving equal weight to opposing positions, regardless of their merit.

The hurricane coverage also reminded us of the remarkable commitment journalists bring to their jobs. Exhibit A is the band of *Times-Picayune* staffers who remained in New Orleans to cover the flooding when their more sensible colleagues evacuated. One who stayed was Brian Thevenot, who recounts their extraordinary experiences in [the *American Journalism Review* in] "Apocalypse in New Orleans." . . .

There's a great moment when—after the levees burst and with water lapping at the *Times-Picayune* building—the brass tells the staff that the plan is to flee to Baton Rouge or Houma, then come back in with the National Guard. That doesn't sit so well with some staffers. Finally, Sports Editor David Meeks asks Editor Jim Amoss for a delivery truck so he can lead a small group of reporters into the fray.

"How are you going to eat?" Amoss asks. "How are you going to file?"

American Media and Celebrities Supported Katrina Relief Efforts

- Cable giant Comcast Corp. said it will donate $50,000 in cash to the Red Cross and another $10 million worth of advertising time on its various channels to encourage charitable donations on behalf of Katrina victims. Comcast-owned E! Networks said it has commitments from such stars as Eva Longoria, Pamela Anderson, Julie Andrews, George Lopez, Mariah Carey, Carlos Santana, and Paula Abdul to appear in public-service announcements encouraging donations to the Red Cross.

- Nicolas Cage donated $1 million to the American Red Cross on Thursday, publicist Annett Wolf said. Cage, who maintains a residence in New Orleans, "wishes to help his neighbors during this most devastating time."

- Dave Matthews Band said it would hold a benefit concert Sept. 12 in Denver to raise funds for various Katrina-related charitable organizations.

- Locally, KABC-TV Los Angeles and its Walt Disney Co.–owned radio siblings have brought in $600,000 for the Red Cross through on-air pitches and fundraising drives held Wednesday at Dodger Stadium in Los Angeles and at the Arrowhead Pond in Anaheim.

- Home-shopping titan QVC and its vendors have pledged to raise $3 million for the Red Cross by donating a portion of QVC sales through Thursday to the Red Cross' hurricane relief fund, with matching corporate contributions from QVC.

Taken from: Cynthia Littleton, "Industry Mobilizes to Aid Victims," *Hollywood Reporter*, September 2, 2005.

Replies Meeks, "Jim, we'll find a way." And they did.

Joining them was Natalie Pompilio, a former *Times-Picayune* reporter who was covering the hurricane for the *Philadelphia Inquirer*. At one point, she and Thevenot interviewed a forlorn bunch of hurricane victims who had been rescued, then abandoned. They were eager, nay desperate, to tell their heartbreaking stories.

After the two journalists got back into their car, Pompilio, an AJR [*American Journalism Review*] contributor, turned to Thevenot and said, "I know it may sound inappropriate, but I love my job on days like this."

SIX

Hurricane Katrina Victims Have Been Forgotten

Deepa Fernandes

Deepa Fernandes is a journalist, author, and host of *Wakeup Call*, a WBAI radio program in New York. She is also the founder of People's Production House, a production institute for youth and immigrant workers. In this viewpoint, written three years after Hurricane Katrina, Fernandes sympathizes with a New Orleans hurricane victim who is trying to recover her life after the disaster. Despite the regrowth of the city, many citizens have been left impoverished and displaced. While the Federal Emergency Management Agency (FEMA) continues to rapidly close its trailer park communities, a lack of jobs and housing options has resulted in a higher-than-normal homeless population. Fernandes reveals the injustice of how the exhaustion of relief funds has left individuals on their own to seek the help they still need.

"That's President Bush hugging me. See how tightly he's hugging me?" It was the chilly end of 2006 in Baker, Louisiana, when Lena Beard asked me this, proudly waving a newspaper clipping my direction as we talked in her still-temporary home. The fading photo, taken the same day the mother of two took refuge on a mattress in a church after

Deepa Fernandes, "Three Years After Hurricane Katrina, Homelessness Looms," *Mother Jones*, August 28, 2008. Reproduced by permission.

Hurricane Katrina, had served as proof after the levees burst that she was going to be okay. "I'm a veteran who has served my country and put my life on the line. I believed my country would take care of me and my family," she said.

But three years after natural disaster stripped Beard and her sons of their house in New Orleans, she is still not okay. Unable to find a place she can afford after being evicted this summer from Renaissance Village, the largest [Federal Emergency Management Agency] (FEMA) trailer park in the country, the Beard family is contemplating a move next month into a homeless shelter.

I first met Beard [in 2006], while she was living in one of the 75,000 toxic trailers issued to Katrina evacuees. Ninety miles from New Orleans, she had grown discouraged and depressed after struggling with a three-hour commute each way trying to find work in her home city. She and her family had occupied the "temporary" shelter since October 2005. The day we met was the first day she had come out of it in a month. "I'm not proud that my children see me staying in bed all day, but I don't know what

One year after Hurricane Katrina, people were still living in FEMA trailers. In 2008 FEMA started shutting down FEMA trailer parks because of high levels of formaldehyde in the structures.

to do. I just don't," she told her neighbors in December 2006, at a residents' meeting of Renaissance Village. "I feel you honey, I feel you," came the sympathetic response. Cold winter winds whipped past the flaps of the big white tent where Beard and the other residents were gathered.

Homes and Jobs Are Hard to Find

Like others in the room, also evacuees from a poor and heavily African American neighborhood in New Orleans, Lena had received a trailer for herself and her two sons. The trailer was approximately 8 foot by 32 foot, with two sectioned-off ends that served as bedrooms. Even if she was watching TV in her room with the flimsy door shut, everyone in the trailer could hear what the other was doing. "My children used to have their own rooms," Beard told me of the home she used to own. "And they both had computers." No one wants to be a homeowner again more than she does.

From February 2007 through the summer months, Beard actively pursued various options to move her family back to New Orleans. She commuted in on weekends to work a bar job on Canal Street, which didn't last long due to health issues that made it hard for her to stand for eight consecutive hours. In July 2007, just one month shy of her two-year displacement anniversary, a final housing option fell through. With no job, and having spent down the last of her savings in the years since the storm, she was unable to come up with the money to cover a security deposit and the first and last months' rent. She was devastated.

But she was not alone. In the years after the storm, moving displaced low-income families back to New Orleans has become less and less realistic. Yes, 92 percent of hotels in New Orleans were open by mid-2007, but by June 2008, 40 percent of public schools remained closed. The number of public buses up and running is still nowhere near pre-Katrina levels.

FEMA Trailers Are Toxic

In the fall of 2007 the number of active trailers still numbered more than 50,000. By February 2008, when CDC [Centers for

Disease Control and Prevention] tests confirmed high levels of formaldehyde in FEMA trailers across Louisiana and Mississippi, FEMA began an aggressive push to shut down its trailer parks and "relocate families into safer and more permanent housing." In the first quarter of 2008, FEMA displaced over 10,000 trailer residents. But even after the formaldehyde scandal had broken, the cramped and toxic trailers were the only security most residents had. "This is home, and I ain't going to move into any slum just because FEMA tell me I have to," Beard lamented to me in early 2008, referring to the apartments FEMA had on its lists of available long-term rentals.

Beard received a knock at her trailer door one June morning and was told she had two days to pack her things. After two days she and her family were moved into a motel and given a month to find alternative accommodation. "I'm so tired from all this," Beard told me then, in the motel room that housed the belongings she was able to salvage from her trailer before being locked out of it. "I just want my family to live in a decent home after all we've been through, so we can rebuild our lives. Is that too much to ask?"

Cartoon by Ed Fischer, www.CartoonStock.com.

This summer, FEMA spokesperson Gina Cortez told *Mother Jones*, "FEMA has closed 106 of its 111 group sites in Louisiana. Renaissance Village is one of them."

Beard's was one of the last five families to leave the trailer park.

FEMA's Help Is Not Enough

Cortez claims FEMA has helped "all eligible trailer residents transition into long-term housing," but ask around the motels where former Renaissance residents have gone after 30 days, and you hear a different story. While some have moved to homes of relatives in other states, others are living in cars, or have joined the rapidly growing New Orleans homeless population.

FEMA reiterates that its mission, beyond meeting emergency needs, is to simply complete infrastructure repairs and return a disaster area to its predisaster state. The agency won't build new housing for displaced residents, even if it could be done for less money than what it costs to temporarily house people, because it's outside their purview. But if FEMA isn't responsible for finding these people housing, who is?

Beard and her family are still scrambling to find out. She had hoped to move into a lovely house with a yard near Renaissance Village—Catholic Charities even paid the landlord a security deposit—and she thought she could afford to move in. But due to what she says is a technical error, FEMA has deemed her ineligible for housing assistance, and as a result the lease fell through. While she searches for housing she can afford, her home state is being rebuilt around her. Her final eviction from the motel will come [in August 2008] just shy of the three-year anniversary when she lost her home to Hurricane Katrina.

SEVEN

The U.S. Response to Disaster Relief Has Improved Since Hurricane Katrina

USA Today

> USA Today is a national American daily newspaper with the widest circulation of any newspaper in the United States. In this viewpoint the editors argue that the U.S. government learned important lessons about disaster relief from Hurricane Katrina in 2005. These lessons were implemented, they say, during Hurricane Gustav, which came ashore along the Gulf Coast in August 2008. Since Katrina, the Federal Emergency Management Agency (FEMA) has improved the way it handles evacuations, its readiness for evacuations, and its spending, which has increased to provide protection to flood zones through repairing and upgrading failed levees. Despite these improvements, the editors warn that Americans should not be lured into a false sense of security. There is still much work to do to protect coastal areas from future storms.

Hurricane Gustav proved [in August 2008] that at least there are some lessons people don't have to learn twice.

"Gustav Reveals Progress, Continuing Vulnerabilities," USA Today, September 2, 2008. Reprinted with permission.

Three years after Hurricane Katrina devastated the Gulf Coast, drowned New Orleans, displaced hundreds of thousands of residents and killed 1,800, the complacency and government ineptitude revealed by that storm have been replaced by better planning, more competence, less cronyism and a healthier respect for the awesome power of nature.

As Gustav moved inland, it looked as if New Orleans had weathered the worst without a repeat of the August 2005 catastrophe. But the storm caused extensive damage elsewhere along the Gulf Coast and [had potential to] trigger major flooding in western Louisiana and eastern Texas.

There was a reticence to let out a sigh of relief too soon this time, as well as other major shifts in attitude. This time, there was no flyover of the devastated area by an aloof President [George W.] Bush looking out the window of Air Force One. This time, Bush canceled his appearance at the Republican National Convention in St. Paul and visited storm shelters in Texas. In fact, Republicans wisely scaled back their carefully choreographed gathering. GOP [Grand Old Party] nominee John McCain recognized that sometimes the best politics is no politics. He flew to Jackson, Miss., for a storm briefing and said it was important to reach out to help "fellow citizens in this time of tragedy and disaster."

The Government Got It Right with Gustav

If anybody deserves that compassion and aid, it is the twice-battered people of the Gulf Coast, who are still healing from the wounds of Katrina and, in many ways, just starting to rebuild. At least they and the nation can take some solace in what went right this time:

Evacuation. As Gustav approached, nearly 2 million fled the coast, urged on by state and local leaders, including New Orleans Mayor Ray Nagin (whose hyperbolic "storm of the century" warning got people's attention but might hurt his credibility the next time around). Before Katrina, not only had the evacuation order come too late, but there was no real way to make it stick in a

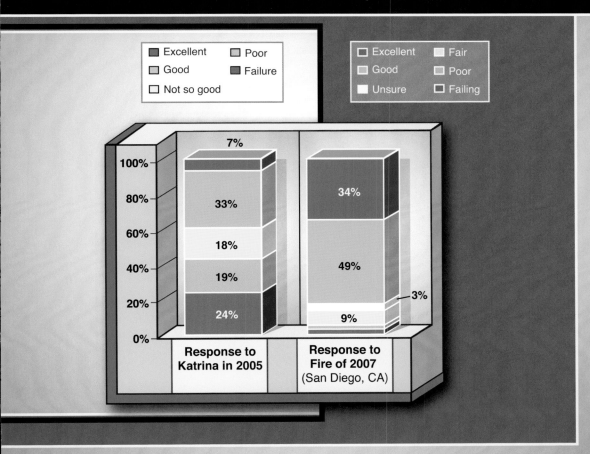

Taken from: John E. Nienstedt, "Wildfires 2007: Things Went Better This Time Around,"
San Diego Institute for Policy Research, November 2007. www.sandiegoinstitute.com.

city where many residents were too poor, too old, too sick or too unworried to leave. This time, residents were bused from neighborhood pickup points to the train station, where buses and trains took them out of harm's way.

Readiness. [In 2005] the Federal Emergency Management Agency proved utterly inept. Little wonder: Its director had worked as a commissioner at an Arabian horse society before his presidential appointment. Today, FEMA's director is a former fire chief with years of experience; his deputy is a retired Coast Guard

The author points to FEMA's handling of the Gulf Coast evacuation in the face of Hurricane Gustav as proof that FEMA has learned valuable lessons from the Katrina disaster.

vice admiral. The agency has been revamped, and that showed in detailed planning. Patients were moved from hospitals. Food, water and rescue teams were ready. Evacuees were allowed to take their pets to avoid the tragedies that occurred when owners stayed behind during Katrina, refusing to abandon beloved cats and dogs.

Protections. Congress and the Bush administration have poured billions of dollars into repairing and upgrading the failed levees. And certainly those levees are stronger. But the topping of the Industrial Canal floodwall was an ominous reminder of the tiny margin for error. In at least one other nearby parish, water was pouring over a levee and lives were at risk.

For all the lessons learned and improvements made, there is much unfinished business. Miles of planned levee upgrades are incomplete. Many residents have been lured by a false sense of safety to rebuild in neighborhoods still at risk. The federal government hasn't begun rebuilding the marshes, swamps and barrier islands so crucial to slowing down storms and protecting the coast. And the federal flood insurance program still promotes risky development in coastal areas.

The nation can be proud of its progress since the international disgrace that was Katrina. But with [other storms] poised to strike the U.S. mainland next, there's no time or place for celebration.

EIGHT

Disaster Relief Efforts Ignore Undocumented Workers

Amanda Martinez

Amanda Martinez is a writer for New America Media, an ethnic news organization. Martinez insists in this viewpoint that undocumented Mexican workers have been over-looked in the relief efforts during the wildfires in California. Martinez expresses her concern that while these workers may be hard to reach either physically or through a language barrier, they should not be forgotten. Relief workers should make a conscious effort to get to these people in times of danger, she says. Another problem Martinez emphasizes is that the Federal Emergency Management Agency (FEMA) is limited in the help it can give to these workers due to their lack of legal documentation. Because they are not legal immigrants, migrant workers oftentimes fear seeking help due to deportation anxiety. Martinez points out that immigrants may not need to worry as workers are always needed to help rebuild after the fires.

The relief efforts in the Southern California [2007] fires have been praised as effective, but they've missed a population that has long been in the shadows: undocumented workers living along San Diego's hillsides and canyons. These men, who represent some of the most essential workers in one of the biggest local industries, have slipped through the cracks in the county's relief and evacuation efforts—so much so that Mexican government officials are filling in the gaps.

"The Mexican Consulate are the ones who have led the relief effort to the farmworkers in the canyons," says Eddie Preciado, director of La Posada de Guadalupe, the only homeless shelter for male farmworkers in San Diego County. He says the consulate has organized partnerships with groups like his in order to conduct searches and provide supplies to the canyon dwellers.

Immigrant advocacy groups are uncertain how these workers are surviving. They say the fires have left the workers scattered and unaccounted for. Evacuation orders have closed off access to these communities, making it very difficult for support teams to assess the population's needs and nearly impossible to determine how many living quarters have been destroyed in the fires.

Migrant Workers Are Isolated from Relief Efforts

The farmworkers are hard to reach physically, living in the remote areas of the canyon, but they are also linguistically isolated. Many are members of Mexico's indigenous Mixtec and Zapotec communities and do not speak English or Spanish.

"Indigenous Mexicans who speak languages such as Mixteco are at high risk of being in danger because they don't understand warnings being given in English or Spanish and they are not likely to trust people unless they are approached speaking their language," says photojournalist David Bacon, who has documented farmworker communities in rural California.

It has been estimated that there are more than 1,600 agricultural workers and day laborers living in the area in makeshift settlements, according to the Regional Task Force on the Homeless in San Diego. This is probably a low estimate of those affected by the fires because it is impossible to know exactly how many workers live this way. Described as "rural homeless," they scrape by without electricity, a water supply or sanitation systems in order to be close to the farms where they work.

Workers Often Resist Relief

These workers make up an essential agricultural labor force in San Diego County, which is one of the top agricultural producers in California and ranks second in the nation in its number of farms, according to the Regional Task Force on the Homeless.

Yet despite the industry's reliance on these laborers, they could be left out of the Federal Emergency Management Agency's [(FEMA)] relief aid because, without papers, they have very limited access to FEMA funds.

Konane Martinez, of the National Latino Research Center, anticipates that documentation will be a requirement for most federal government agencies providing relief in the area. As a result, Martinez is collaborating with eighteen different organizations to collect money and resources for displaced farmworkers looking for aid once the fires subside.

"I don't think anyone will be turned away from immediate assistance," says Dorothy Johnson, an attorney with California Legal Rural Assistance, which provides farmworkers with legal support. And though no one has reported being denied help, many undocumented immigrants are not seeking aid because they do not know which rescue workers they can trust. Many see the risk of deportation as more dangerous than the fires themselves.

"I wouldn't be surprised if they avoided firefighters," says Bacon, adding that many undocumented workers are wary of law enforcement for fear of being detained or deported. "Many of these workers have experienced intense situations of danger just to get into the United States" and earn money to send to their families back home, explains Bacon. They are willing to endure very harsh conditions, he says, to avoid being caught by Border Patrol or Immigration and Customs Enforcement (ICE) agents.

Some Immigrants Have Stayed Behind

The Spanish-language publication *Enlace*, in San Diego, reported that some farmworkers have chosen to remain in the canyons despite warnings to evacuate because they do not want to leave.

Illegal immigrant farmworkers in California are often underserved by government relief agencies because of fear of deportation if they seek help.

Meanwhile, some who do are not being allowed to leave. "Some farmers are not following evacuation orders and have kept workers in the fields despite orders being given to evacuate," says Christian Ramirez of the American Friends Service Committee.

But if they stay they should know that, as Ramirez explains, "the atmosphere conditions are not safe to be working in." His organization has been sending volunteers into the fields to supply farmworkers with eye drops, face masks and goggles.

The Border Patrol Is Not to Be Feared

Apparently unconcerned that the use of Border Patrol agents might discourage undocumented residents from seeking help,

Governor Arnold Schwarzenegger called on the US Border Patrol to help with the emergency relief efforts. Matthew Johnson says about 300 agents are now "watching for looters, monitoring affected neighborhoods and safety control" during the fire relief efforts.

Some agents were working alongside local police when six undocumented immigrants were arrested [in October 2007] outside Qualcomm Stadium, one of the main fire relief sites. Those arrested were reportedly seen stealing relief supplies consisting of fold-up cots and bottles of water from Qualcomm. Police Sgt. Jesse Cesena told the San Diego *Union-Tribune* that "they were stealing from the people in need." The police turned the immigrants over to Border Patrol agents.

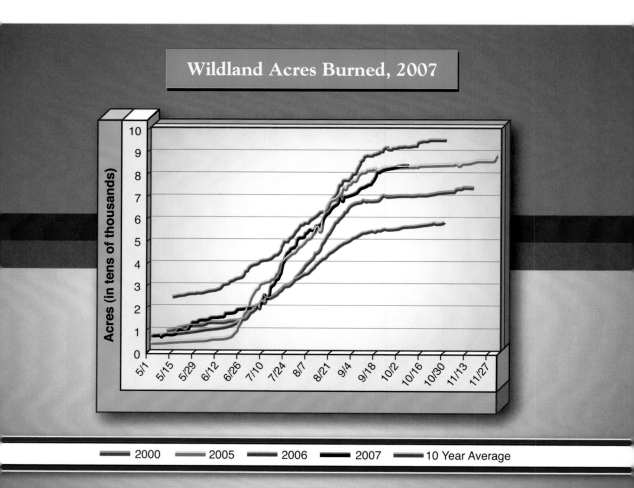

Wildland Acres Burned, 2007

Acres (in tens of thousands)

2000   2005   2006   2007   10 Year Average

Taken from: National Incident Information Center, www.fs.fed.us/news/fire.

Although Border Patrol agents are busy with local relief efforts, Johnson says they are still watching the border. Since the start of the fires, he says, they have apprehended 900 immigrants trying to cross into the United States.

Ironically, Leo Estrada, professor of urban planning at UCLA, believes the undocumented workers shouldn't worry. Immigration and Customs Enforcement (ICE) won't be conducting raids anytime soon, he says.

In fact, he predicts, immigrant workers will be needed in reconstruction efforts after the fire. More than 410,000 acres of land have burned, and clean-up efforts will be critical. "With more than 1,000 homes being demolished," he notes, "contractors will be looking to immigrant labor forces to demolish, cart away and rebuild houses."

"We saw it in New Orleans," says Estrada. Undocumented immigrants from Mexico and Central America were among the largest groups employed in rebuilding the city after Hurricane Katrina.

"At the time of reconstruction, nobody bothered them. It will be interesting to see," says Estrada. "They will be bringing back a labor force they have been trying to get rid of."

NINE

Pets Should Not Be Forgotten During Natural Disasters

Laura Bevan

> Laura Bevan is the director of the Southeast Regional Office of the Humane Society of the United States, which is located in Tallahassee, Florida. In this viewpoint Bevan urges animal owners to plan for their pets' safety in the event of an emergency, such as a natural disaster. If an evacuation is ordered, owners should take their pets with them, instructs Bevan. In the event that shelter must be taken inside a house, Bevan advises owners to choose a room where all people and animals can stay together. A plan for retrieving animals in the event of an emergency when no one is home is also important for pet owners to consider.

In the overwhelming tragedy of the terrorist attacks of Sept. 11, 2001, while workers frantically tried to find and save possible survivors in the rubble, another rescue effort was underway as well. In the evacuated apartments surrounding Ground Zero, companion animals waited faithfully for the return of their displaced families. These owners had left for work that morning, never comprehending the horror that would change the fate of so many in such a short time, never knowing as they petted and/

or murmured goodbyes to their beloved dog, cat, rabbit, bird, etc. that soon the animals would be frantic for their safe return.

Over the next few days, rescue workers from local agencies escorted people through police barricades into damaged buildings to be reunited with their companion animals, or took keys to enter apartments to retrieve frightened and hungry pets. As a result, few animals died in relation to the attacks, and families who were already reeling in shock were spared that additional grief.

Most Americans were probably unaware of efforts to save the animal victims of the World Trade Center attack, but few natural or manmade disasters in this country have been without animal victims. More than half the families in America have pets. When disaster strikes, the safety and lives of those animals are threatened. Rescue doesn't always come in time, so it is vital that those of us who share our lives with companion animals plan for their safety during evacuations, when sheltering at home, or even when we are not available ourselves.

Don't be fooled into thinking that you won't be a victim of a disaster. There is no place in this country, or any other for that matter, that is immune. Hurricanes, floods, wildfires, winter storms, earthquakes, hazardous material spills, and now terrorist attacks are all possibilities, and the nightly news is filled with stories of people who thought it would never happen to them. Hope that it never happens to you, but with disaster plans for your entire family, including pets, you will be prepared if your luck doesn't hold out.

If You Evacuate, Take Your Pets with You

I grew up in Florida with its annual threat of hurricanes. The refrain at that time was, if an evacuation was ordered, the humans got in the car and went to a safe shelter, while dogs, cats, or other pets were locked in the bathroom with three days of food and water where they could be safe. Of course, it never occurred to us to consider what was so magical about our bathrooms that they would protect our animals when they were not safe for us.

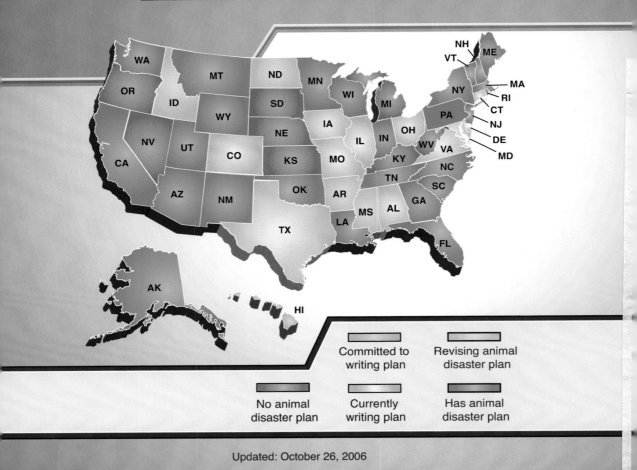

Animal Disaster Plans of U.S. States

Committed to writing plan

Revising animal disaster plan

No animal disaster plan

Currently writing plan

Has animal disaster plan

Updated: October 26, 2006

Taken from: Friends of Animals, www.friendsofanimals.org.

In 1992, the fallacy of that message came home in the guise of Hurricane Andrew. As it gained in strength and honed in on the area south of Miami, hundreds of thousands of people heeded the dire warnings of authorities and fled to evacuation shelters, hotels/motels, and the homes of family and friends. The message to "leave your pet at home" was repeated on television and radio, and the panicked masses dutifully complied. On the morning of Aug. 24, Andrew came ashore with winds gusting up to 177 miles per hour. Tens of thousands of residences were torn apart, and an estimated 170,000 people were left homeless. Animals were caught up in the storm and blown away, were buried in the remains of their former homes, or ran terrorized through devastated neighborhoods. Many were killed or wounded terribly by flying debris and collapsing buildings.

In the aftermath, as the human survivors slowly pulled themselves from the rubble, so did their companion animals. Some stayed in place waiting for their owners' return; others, frightened by a world that was no longer familiar, began a search for nourishment and comfort. As they wandered, they became victims of cars, other animals, contaminated food and water, or accidents.

For the next two months, I joined an array of good Samaritans from around Florida and the rest of the country in a quest to help the homeless pets of Andrew. Over 600 of the thousands of lost dogs and cats found safety and a new life in our compound, which was composed of Army tents and surrounded by recreation vehicles and camping facilities. Some companion animals were reunited with their owners, but most were not. Every day was filled with tearful people standing in line under the hot sun, clutching at the hope that their pet had found its way to our compound.

Thousands of reports were filled out concerning lost pets, and each had its own sorrow-soaked story. Branded into my memory is the father who evacuated his wife and children to a shelter, leaving behind three cats locked in the bathroom of their mobile home. After the storm, he frantically tried to retrieve the cats, only to find the home and all its neighbors completely gone. As he looked through the book of photos of cats that we had provided haven for, his voice broke as he spoke of his wife and children's non-ending grief for their pets. He returned to the compound several times in the following weeks, but, despite the large number of cats rescued from the destroyed mobile home parks, none were the right ones for his family.

In the years since Hurricane Andrew, the message to the public has slowly changed. Now the message is: If it is dangerous for you, it is dangerous for your pets; if you care about them, take them with you. In the planning that each family should already be doing for its human members, planning ahead for companion animals isn't that much more time or effort.

Shelter in Your Own Home If That Is the Safest Option

In 1999, more than 2,500,000 people evacuated in the face of Hurricane Floyd, which was the size of Texas and just as powerful as Andrew. Major interstates and highways in Florida, Georgia, and South Carolina became virtual parking lots. Car trips that required two hours on a normal day took 18 hours of bumper-to-bumper traffic, with evacuees all trying to get somewhere safe at the same time. If Hurricane Floyd had not swerved, becoming North Carolina's worst nightmare, thousands of people and pets could have been trapped by the storm in their cars and been killed or seriously injured.

In this and other cases, such as tornadoes, families may decide or be forced to shelter in place. If you are, choose a room in your home where the entire family, including animals, can stay together. If possible, put animals in crates to keep them calm and lessen the chance they will escape if the room is damaged. For large dogs, leashing might be the best option. Keep pet food, medications, and water inside watertight containers along with your emergency supplies.

For me, my "safe room" is a windowless bathroom in the center of my house. It is large enough to hold the crates of my four dogs, one cat, and one bird and has a small closet where I keep my stockpiled supplies, important papers, and photographs. One of my goals is to hurricane-shutter all the windows and make sure the house in general is as secure as possible. After seeing the destruction of Andrew, I have to do everything I can to minimize the chance that I will be a victim of such a disaster. Two of my dogs have already been disaster victims— Pepper came from the Andrew compound, while Shorty was unclaimed after the Georgia floods of 1994. I owe it to them to keep them safe.

What Will Happen If You Are Not Home and a Disaster Occurs in Your Community?

In 1996, a train hauling propane tanks overturned near the town of Weyauwega, Wis. Many residents had already left for work and were blocked from returning when they tried to get back to their pets. At first, they were told that they would be displaced for a short time, but, as the hours turned into days, animal owners became more upset and militant. Residents defied barricades to sneak back into town at night to rescue animals, and the Governor's office was flooded with calls from around the country demanding support for a pet rescue effort. Finally, armored military vehicles took residents and animal workers into the quarantined area to retrieve pets.

Contrast that with the situation in New Mexico in May, 2000, when a controlled burn near Los Alamos exploded into a major

A woman readies her dog for evacuation from Hurricane Gustav. Pet owners must take care of their pets before evacuating and ensure they are not left behind.

wildfire that threatened several towns in the area. More than 25,000 people were evacuated, and many were unable to return home to retrieve their companion animals. This time, the community had a plan, and pet owners were notified that rescue teams were close by. Armed with keys and directions for locating the pets, the teams drove into no-entry zones to save hundreds of animals from a horrifying death. Temporary animal shelters were set up to handle over 700 displaced pets that eventually were reunited with their relieved families.

To protect the safety of your companion animals when you are not home, make arrangements well in advance with a trusted neighbor to take your pets and meet you at a specific location. Be sure he or she has a key to your home and knows your animals, where they stay in the house, and where your disaster supply kit is located.

If no one is available to evacuate your pets, notify authorities. Check with your local animal control or humane society to see if it is coordinating animal rescues. Local disaster relief agencies—such as the American Red Cross and the Salvation Army—often have information on animal rescue efforts and can give you contact numbers. If the animal is inside, get a house key to rescuers along with the best information possible on the pet's location. Many creatures, especially cats, will hide when afraid and will not come out to strangers. In situations like the World Trade Center attack, knowing which apartments contained pets meant the difference between them being rescued or left abandoned in the buildings.

Disasters of any cause or proportion are synonymous with loss and sorrow, as homes, jobs, and communities are destroyed and people's lives are changed forever. However, the loss or injury of a beloved pet doesn't have to occur. By planning now, you can minimize or eliminate the danger. Having a plan isn't a guarantee that nothing bad will ever happen, but it does mean that you and your companion animals have a better chance of surviving and staying together.

If you share your life with animals, take a look into their trusting eyes tonight and make a promise that if you do not already have plans to protect yourself and them, you will soon. In the end, your pets' safety depends on you.

TEN

International Policy Is Needed to Humanely Provide Disaster Relief to Reluctant Countries

Michael Moran

Michael Moran is an executive editor and writer at the Council on Foreign Relations' Web site, cfr.org. Moran claims in this viewpoint that an immense difference is apparent in the way China and Myanmar handled their 2008 earthquake disasters. While China let both the media and relief workers into the country, Myanmar kept both out. Moran maintains that this caused tens of thousands of people in Myanmar to die when post-disaster disease began to flourish. He wonders if countries in similar situations should be forced to take relief for the sake of their people. Moran is quick to point out that relief is not always helpful; however, he says that nations of all sizes must realize that they need help in times of disaster.

The path of devastation cut by Cyclone Nargis in Myanmar [in May 2008] appears now likely to have extinguished more than 100,000 lives. Natural disasters have a way of reminding humans how helpless they can be when pitted against nature, and an earthquake that killed at least 55,000 in southwestern China 10 days later added unwelcome emphasis to the point.

China's tragedy also took the spotlight off Myanmar, in part because journalists are actually able to cover the Chinese tragedy, whereas Myanmar's military junta [the group controlling the government] has prevented not only international journalists but international relief agencies from entering the country in any great numbers. U.N. Secretary-General Ban Ki-moon won a pledge from the dictatorial regime late last week to open up to foreign aid, but it is still to be tested, and it comes after weeks of unfathomable, inexcusable stalling.

The context of these two tragedies, the differing ways they have been handled by their respective authoritarian governments, is worth pondering. China deserves enormous praise for opening up to international assistance, apparently internalizing the lessons of previous crises, most notably the 2005 bird flu outbreak, when Beijing's stonewalling allowed a containable problem to get out of hand. Good precedents have been set.

Yet in foreign policy, economic and scientific terms, the fallout from the cyclone in Myanmar holds far more serious implications. Outsiders fume at a regime so fearful for its own survival that it would allow tens of thousands more of its citizens to perish of post-disaster disease, exposure and privations, rather than allow a willing world to come help. This has led to an important debate in foreign policy circles: Is the behavior of Myanmar's generals so irresponsible that it justifies the use of force to save its citizens? And did the existence of this threat help the U.N. chief pry open Myanmar's borders to aid workers?

Relief Raises Questions

The philosophical questions are easier to manage, of course. Put simply, does a decision to forgo international assistance, and by extension condemn thousands to die, amount to a crime against humanity? Judged by Western standards, preventing all possible aid is criminal. But the relevant standards here are Asian, remember, then international, and only after that, Western. The debate rages against a backdrop of a relatively new United Nations doctrine known as "the Responsibility to Protect."

R2P, as U.N. wonks refer to it, grew out of the inaction of the international community during the 1994 Rwanda genocide and, in short, establishes a "right to humanitarian intervention" when a sovereign government has failed to act to protect its own people.

But protect them from what? This is the crux of the debate. Currently, R2P is understood by most to apply primarily in cases involving genocide or organized violence. Ramesh Thakur, a vice rector at the United Nations University in Tokyo and a member of the U.N. panel that drew up R2P, says a specific reference to natural disasters was removed because of the objections of some member states when the doctrine was promulgated in 2005.

Pallets of medical supplies await shipment to China's earthquake victims. The Chinese government allowed workers and supplies into their country, but Myanmar's ruling junta did not and caused greater loss of life.

To many, with thousands of lives at stake, this sounds mealy-mouthed. Both the United States and France have ships capable of mounting rescue operations stationed off the Myanmar coastline. But entreaties to the generals were, until this week, rebuffed, leading French Foreign Minister Bernard Kouchner to demand the U.N. invoke R2P to authorize airdrops. Even now, the ability of experienced Western aid workers to operate inside the cyclone zone remains in question.

What Is a Cyclone?

A tropical cyclone is the generic term for a low pressure system over tropical or sub-tropical waters, with organized convection (i.e., thunderstorm activity) and winds at low levels, circulating either anti-clockwise (in the northern hemisphere) or clockwise (in the southern hemisphere). The terms *hurricane* and *typhoon* are regionally specific names for a strong tropical cyclone.

Tropical cyclones with maximum sustained surface winds of less than 39 mph are called **tropical depressions**. Once the winds around the tropical cyclone reach at least 39 mph it is called a **tropical storm** and is assigned a name. If winds reach 74 mph, then it is a called a:

- **hurricane** – in the North Atlantic Ocean and the northeast Pacific Ocean, east of the dateline;

- **typhoon** – in the northwest Pacific Ocean, west of the dateline;

- **tropical cyclone** – in other regions, including the Indian Ocean and South Pacific Ocean.

Taken from: Met Office, "Tropical Cyclone Facts," www.metoffice.gov.uk.

Relief Not Always Helpful

Beyond the question of approval from the government of the stricken country, the mounting of any kind of humanitarian operation invariably raises difficult questions for those involved. The American military's capabilities, already overstretched in Iraq and Afghanistan, are vital to such operations.

The specter of past failures looms large. Think back to 1992. In December of that year, almost a year to the day that the Soviet Union disbanded itself and released the world from the policy straitjacket of the Cold War, 1,800 U.S. Marines landed on an East African beach in Somalia, where chaos reigned and several million faced starvation.

The "invasion" was unusual in a number of respects: Ordered by President George H.W. Bush a month after his defeat by Bill Clinton but before the new president took office; announced ahead of time, rather than kept secret. Yet the mission's most significant oddity was its billing as a "humanitarian intervention," a deployment of the battle-hardened U.S. military that had just won the first Gulf War for "operations other than combat," as military jargon puts it. The president told the nation the military was being sent, along with international allies, "to do God's work."

As we now know, the operation turned out to include plenty of combat, and ever since the military has furiously resisted such missions. Even though the first phase of "Operation Restore Hope" did end the famine and, briefly, calm the clan and ethnic violence that afflicts Somalia, that is not the mission's legacy. Instead, "Black Hawk Down" is how the mission is remembered, followed by an ignominious retreat. "Somalia" took its place with "Vietnam" and "Beirut" as one-word repellents against certain kinds of American military missions abroad.

Help Still Needed Despite Problems

That has not kept America's military from making the difference between life and death for Asians in past disasters, most recently in the 2004 tsunami and the 2006 earthquake in Pakistan. But even during the tsunami, Indonesia initially told the United States to stay away, and India never permitted foreign aid workers to come in.

Intervening on principle, then, is not the current template: As Myanmar's generals have proven, help requires an invitation. And even with one, as in Pakistan, the much ballyhooed "good feelings" toward America such missions are supposed to engender rarely materialize. The thankless nature of the task should be faced at the outset.

Still, perhaps what the outside world may be able to hope for in Myanmar's suffering is a re-evaluation of R2P to include nations overwhelmed by nature. Even today, convincing many countries once ruled by the "civilizing white man" to allow that kind of access may prove impossible.

ASEAN [the Association of Southeast Asian Nations], the regional economic grouping that met [in May 2008] to discuss the Myanmar crisis, said as much in its final statement. Myanmar had hoped to limit foreign aid workers to ASEAN nations, all of which have proven loath to criticize the junta's human rights abuses. Meanwhile, longer-term challenges highlighted in the Irrawaddy Delta also need serious attention. If climate-change scientists are even half right, these kinds of events, especially in low-lying coastal nations, are a growing threat, not just an oddity. Even aggressive action on climate change may not be able to forestall rising seas in the next decades. The capability to manage such change exists, but, as usual, mostly in the places that least need it.

Separately, the world's policies on food—the trade-distorting agricultural subsidies of the United States and Europe, and the shoddy practices of American food aid programs—need to be revisited quickly. Myanmar's rice crop normally exceeds local demand and helps feed the destitute in Bangladesh and Sri Lanka. That won't happen this year [2008], and the result could be a famine, and political instability, in a region that on any given day is moments away from catastrophe. It may be too late for many in Myanmar, but an intelligent reappraisal of these issues could save millions in the future.

ELEVEN

The United Nations' Humanitarian Relief Efforts Need Oversight

Nile Gardiner

> Nile Gardiner is the director of the Margaret Thatcher Center for Freedom, the Heritage Foundation, a research and educational institute whose mission is to formulate and promote conservative public policies. In the following viewpoint Gardiner discusses the amount of humanitarian aid that was contributed to tsunami relief after the 2004 tsunami in Southeast Asia, and he notes the way in which it was spent. Gardiner argues that Congress should investigate the United Nations' management of the tsunami relief effort because of alarming information about mismanagement gathered in an investigation by the *Financial Times*. Gardiner recommends congressional hearings and investigations to examine this mismanagement; he believes the UN should account for their expenditures; and he suggests that disaster relief funds should be withheld from the UN in the future.

[D]ecember 26, 2005,] marks the anniversary of the tsunami disaster which struck large sections of Southeast Asia, South Asia, and East Africa on December 26, 2004. The tsunami claimed some 231,000 lives and displaced 2 million people. The disaster prompted an outpouring of humanitarian help from around the world, with an estimated total of $13.6 billion in aid pledged, including $6.16 billion in government assistance, $2.3 billion from international financial institutions, and $5.1 billion from individuals and companies.

The huge international relief effort is being co-coordinated by the United Nations, and involves an astonishing 39 U.N. agencies, from the United Nations Children's Fund (UNICEF) and United Nations Educational, Scientific and Cultural Organization (UNESCO), to the World Health Organization (WHO) and the International Labour Organization (ILO).

The *Financial Times* Inquiry

When the U.N. took over the tsunami relief operation in early 2005, the world body pledged full transparency, in light of its disastrous handling of the Iraq Oil-for-Food Program. The U.N.'s under-secretary general for humanitarian affairs, Jan Egeland, boasted in an opinion editorial that "only the UN has the universal legitimacy, capacity, and credibility to lead in a truly global humanitarian emergency." Egeland had earlier criticized the U.S. contribution to the tsunami relief effort as "stingy."

An investigation by the *Financial Times* (*FT*), however, has raised serious questions regarding the U.N.'s handling of the tsunami relief effort, in particular the way in which it has spent the first $590 million of its $1.1 billion disaster "flash appeal." The appeal includes nearly $50 million from the United States. The two-month *FT* inquiry revealed that "as much as a third of the money raised by the UN for its tsunami response was being swallowed up by salaries and administrative overheads." In contrast, Oxfam, a British-based private charity, spent just 10 percent of the tsunami aid money it raised on administrative costs.

Unable to obtain figures from the U.N. Office for the Coordination of Humanitarian Affairs (OCHA), the *FT* approached several U.N. agencies directly to establish exact numbers for tsunami relief expenditure. Many "declined or ignored" requests for information, while others offered incomplete data. The newspaper found that of the $49 million spent by the World

Funds Committed by Foreign Countries to Tsunami Aid as of October 2005

1.	United States	$792,000,000
2.	Japan	$601,000,000
3.	Germany	$313,000,000
4.	France	$243,000,000
5.	Australia	$193,000,000
6.	Canada	$176,000,000
7.	Netherlands	$156,000,000
8.	United Kingdom	$149,000,000
9.	Norway	$139,000,000
10.	Spain	$114,000,000
11.	Italy	$94,000,000
12.	Sweden	$86,000,000
13.	Finland	$44,000,000
14.	Denmark	$41,000,000
15.	New Zealand	$37,000,000
16.	Greece	$33,000,000
17.	Belgium	$30,000,000
18.	Switzerland	$29,000,000
19.	Austria	$28,000,000
20.	Ireland	$26,000,000
21.	Portugal	$13,000,000
22.	Luxembourg	$11,000,000
	Total	**$3,348,000,000**

Taken from: Organisation for Economic Co-operation and Development, "Disaster Statistics," October 2005.

Health Organization as part of the tsunami appeal, 32 percent had been spent on "personnel costs, administrative overheads, or associated 'miscellaneous' costs." At the World Food Program (WFP), 18 percent of the $215 million spent by the agency went toward "staff salaries, administrative overheads and vehicles and equipment."

The *Financial Times* concluded that "a year after the tsunami, pledges of transparency and accountability for the UN's appeal appear a long way from being realized. This is primarily blamed on dueling UN bureaucracies and accounting methods plus what in many cases appears to be institutional paranoia about disclosure."

Accountability and Transparency Are Needed at the U.N.

The *FT*'s findings should raise significant concern over the U.N.'s ability to manage a huge, multi-billion dollar humanitarian relief

Former president Bill Clinton speaks to the United Nations on his assessment of the tsunami recovery programs and the need to address deficiencies within them.

operation. The last such operation that the U.N. oversaw, the Oil-for-Food Program, was an unmitigated failure. The investigations into the scandal by the Security Council–appointed Independent Inquiry Committee (IIC), in addition to several congressional committees and U.S. federal agencies, cast a spotlight on widespread corruption, mismanagement and incompetence within the U.N., and exposed a deeply rooted culture of secrecy at the heart of the United Nations Secretariat. The scandal gravely tarnished the image of the world body as well as its leadership, including Secretary General Kofi Annan.

The Oil-for-Food revelations coincided with a wave of other U.N. scandals, including widespread abuse of refugees by U.N. peacekeepers in the Congo, sexual harassment at the top of the United Nations Refugee Agency (UNHCR) and the United Nations Electoral Assistance Division (EAD), and significant corruption at the U.N. World Meteorological Organization (WMO), all of which seriously damaged the U.N.'s global standing.

With public confidence at an all-time low, it is imperative that both Congress and the George W. Bush Administration seek assurances that U.S. and international donations for tsunami relief are both properly spent and accounted for.

Key Recommendations

Congressional Hearings and Investigations. Both the House and Senate should hold hearings on the U.N.'s management of the tsunami relief program and call for senior U.N. officials, including Jan Egeland, to testify before Congress. The Senate Permanent Subcommittee on Investigations, chaired by Senator Norm Coleman (R-MN), and the newly created House International Relations Subcommittee on Oversight and Investigations, headed by Congressman Dana Rohrabacher (R-CA), should strongly consider extending their investigations into the Oil-for-Food Program to the U.N. tsunami relief operation.

Bush Administration Pressure. The White House and State Department should call on the U.N. to give a full accounting of all its expenditures on tsunami relief operations, including its payments to international aid consultants, who are paid as much as $10,000 a month. All U.N. expenditures on relief efforts should be made publicly available and open to scrutiny.

Withhold Funds From the United Nations. The growing doubts over the U.N.'s handling of the tsunami relief operation reinforce the need for Congress to withhold funds from the U.N.'s assessed budget unless a series of reform measures are implemented by the world body. These must include the establishment of an independent oversight body for the U.N., a far greater degree of openness and transparency, as well as independent auditing procedures.

The growing scandal over the U.N.'s handling of the tsunami "flash appeal" should set off alarm bells in Washington. A picture is beginning to emerge of yet another U.N. operation mired in secrecy, hugely lacking in transparency and oversight, and without a doubt open to widespread mismanagement and corruption. It is increasingly clear that the U.N. has learned little from the Oil-for-Food scandal, and is continuing to operate in a fashion that is out of step with the expectations of U.S. taxpayers, who fund the U.N. to the tune of $3 billion a year.

Both Congress and the Bush Administration must demand answers from the U.N. bureaucracy, and expect that all donations are spent appropriately. It is imperative that tsunami relief go directly to the impoverished victims of the disaster, and not be used to subsidize the salaries or administrative overheads of a vast army of U.N. bureaucrats and consultants. A clear signal must be sent from Washington that any misuse of international funds will not be tolerated. If it is to maintain the long-term support of the United States, the United Nations will have to be substantially reformed and must operate as an efficient, honest, and accountable public body.

TWELVE

Religious Organizations' Volunteers Make a Difference to Disaster Relief

Ted Olsen

> Ted Olsen is the news director and online managing editor at *Christianity Today*, an organization and magazine founded by the Rev. Billy Graham. The nondenominational organization maintains a conservative religious stance but argues for liberal approaches to social problems. In this viewpoint Olsen argues that religious organizations contributed enormously to disaster relief efforts after Hurricane Katrina. Olsen disagrees with other journalists who claim that disasters only inspire onetime giving or that religious groups may have ulterior motives behind their contributions. He contends that Christians are used to giving. Religious organizations are often the first relief groups at the scene of a disaster, he says, not to further their own cause, but as an act of love.

"We've got to stop the flow of water," Seventh-day Adventist disaster services director Charlene Sargent told the *Los Angeles Times* two weeks after Hurricane Katrina struck land. She wasn't talking about broken levees, but about the truckloads of donated drinking water. "If you took everything we got this

Ted Olsen, "The Katrina Quandary: America Questions the Role of Christian Charity," *Christianity Today*, vol. 49, November 2005, p. 94. Reproduced by permission of the author.

weekend and put it in New Orleans," she said, "it would raise the elevation so it wouldn't flood again."

In the first week after Katrina, U.S. charities raised over $500 million—more than 2.5 times the cost of the Louisiana Purchase, adjusted for inflation. Within three weeks, American giving surpassed $1 billion, and in less than four, it had surpassed the to-date gifts for victims of [2004's] Asian tsunami. And that was just what got on the books—it doesn't count the Houston families who rushed to the Astrodome offering housing and food, nor the kindhearted Good Samaritans who loaded up whatever they could find and drove as far into Louisiana as they could.

The Katrina donations may herald a new revolution in giving, said *The Christian Science Monitor*. "People want to participate in a charity walk or hand out sandwiches at a shelter," Stacy Palmer, editor of *The Chronicle of Philanthropy*, told the paper. "They want to take their involvement way beyond just writing a check."

The Downside of Giving

The Washington Post personal finance columnist Michelle Singletary wonders if donors are being trained to respond to news crises rather than to develop a long-term spirit of giving. "While it's commendable that so many people are helping Katrina victims, it's better if that generosity becomes ingrained," she said.

No, it's not, says columnist and cartoonist Ted Rall in one of Katrina's most surprising articles, "Charities Are for Suckers." "Generosity feeds into the mindset of the sinister ideologues who argue that government shouldn't help people," he wrote. "It's time to 'starve the beast': private charities used by the government to justify the abdication of its duties to its citizens."

The Boston Globe columnist James Carroll doesn't go that far, but he agrees that "when religiously sponsored good works supply essential needs in place of government responses, something essential to democracy is at stake. . . . Citizens in a democracy, after all, are the owners of government; therefore government help is a form of self-help."

The author of this viewpoint contends that Christian groups are often among the first charitable organizations on the scene of a disaster and contribute enormously to relief efforts.

Others were outraged that the initial government list of aid organizations was, in the words of *Bloomberg News*, "dominated by religious organizations and exclude[d] many secular and international relief groups." In the *San Francisco Chronicle*, David L. Kirp accused FEMA [the Federal Emergency Management Agency] of discriminating against nonreligious charities. Some, like *The Atlanta Journal-Constitution*'s Diane Glass, warned of religious groups' "ulterior motive": "They may provide assistance to those

Important Reasons for Backing Faith-Based Programs

	Important Reason	Not an Important Reason	Don't Know
People should have a variety of options	77%	20%	3%
Service providers are more caring and compassionate	72%	25%	3%
Power of religion can change people's lives	62%	35%	3%
Faith-based programs are more efficient	60%	36%	4%

Taken from: The Pew Research Center for the People and the Press, "Faith-Based Funding Backed, but Church-State Doubts Abound," April 10, 2001. http://people-press.org.

in need, but they aren't 'in it' to help so much as to amass obedient followers."

Christians Are Used to Giving

Actually, Katrina showed the value of the much-disparaged "organized religion," said Ray Waddle in *The Tennessean*. If faith without works is dead, he said, "organized religion is showing America what it means to believe." Indeed, a headline in *The New York Times* read, "A New Meaning for 'Organized Religion': It Helps the Needy Quickly."

Churches have become first responders because "they're already there," researcher Bryan Jackson told the *Times*. "They represent a focal point in the community."

But it's not just that they're already there. They're already giving. "It is impossible to doubt that faith and charity go hand in
hand," Roy Hattersley wrote in *The Guardian*. "The only possible
conclusion is that faith comes with a packet of moral imperatives
that, while they do not condition the attitude of all believers,
influence enough of them to make them morally superior to athe-
ists like me. The truth may make us free. But it has not made us
as admirable as the average captain in the Salvation Army."

But it's not about imperatives, per se. Christians are used to
giving not because they have to (there is no church tax), nor
even because there is a need. We give because of who we are:
people created in the image of God to give, for giving is an act of
love. We were made to give. And one of the beautiful outcomes
of Katrina's terrible devastation is that Americans have shared in
this blessing, this common grace.

THIRTEEN

Disaster Relief Should Aim to Improve Lives Instead of Simply Restoring Them

Alex Steffen

> Alex Steffen is the executive editor and CEO of *World Changing*, a nonprofit online magazine about sustainability. Steffen believes that poor victims of natural disasters should not be assisted in simply regaining their former circumstances, but could be better helped by improving their overall quality of life. In this viewpoint he argues that the use of innovative materials such as compostable tents for shelter and solar panels, instead of generators, can make relief efforts more effective and efficient and survivor living conditions more habitable with the added benefit of being environmentally friendly.

What if relief and reconstruction efforts aimed not just to save, but to improve the lives of the victims of this week's [December 26, 2004, tsunami] disaster?

This might not seem like the time to look ahead. The situation all around the Indian Ocean is grim: the bulldozers are digging mass-graves for as many as 100,000 bodies; at least a million people are homeless, hungry and utterly destitute; clean water and sanitation facilities don't exist; disease is beginning to break out; and relief is still far off for too, too many people. This is a full-blown global crisis.

But this is exactly the right time for foresight. For one thing, history shows that the world tends to lose interest in disasters in the developing world once people stop dying in large numbers. If we don't think now about our commitment to helping these communities recover and rebuild after the immediate crisis has passed, we never will.

And the ruined cities and villages lining the shores of the Indian Ocean are now home to some of the poorest of the world's poor. In many places, traumatized people, who had very little with which to earn their livelihoods to begin with, now have nothing left at all. Add to this the long-term challenges they face—like decimated local economies, massive pollution (and some new industrial accidents), declining fisheries and forests, lack of capital and, perhaps most ominously, the rising seas and catastrophic storms they can expect from global warming—and their fate may not be an enviable one.

Helping to Change Lives

But that fate is not written in stone. We can still change it. What if [we] didn't just do something to help, but did the right things, and did them fully? What if we looked at this relief and reconstruction effort as a chance to not only save lives (and of course that must come first) but to truly rebuild coastal Southeast Asia along more sustainably prosperous lines? What if we made the commitment to take what are now some of the most ravaged, destitute areas on Earth, and worked with the people there to reimagine and rebuild their communities to be the cutting edge of sustainable development?

What if we made not just relief but rebirth the new measure of our success?

There are reasons to believe we could do it.

Delivering relief aid is a job of staggering proportions in a disaster of this size, and it will continue for months. As I've written before, the demands we put on aid workers are insane. "They have to fly in to remote corners of the Earth, where nothing, not even clean water, can usually be expected, and create an entire city from scratch, restoring order, throwing up tents, digging latrines, finding and filtering water, treating the wounded and diseased, counseling the grieving, and finding ways to bring shell-shocked people back to emotional engagement with their own lives. This is perhaps the hardest work on Earth, and the people who do it—the bluehats and doctors without borders, the aid workers and missionaries—are the closest thing we have to unquestionable heroes."

Building Adequate Shelter

Let's give them tools to do their jobs better. Innovate and improve the relief effort, right now, from the start. Take ahold of the best innovations around and spread them as quickly as possible: employ better logistics methods, get aid workers better information about conditions on the ground and provide better and smarter disaster medical care to the victims.

Refugee camps can themselves become engines of transformation. At least a million have been made refugees by this tragedy: we can reinvent the refugee camp, and turn it into a launching pad for reconstruction.

We can't yet expect camps like this—

One possibility is the compostable tent city. In this model, the tents themselves would be treated cardboard shelters—like Icopods (which resemble paper geodesic domes)—which provide basic shelter and last for a couple years. The shipping containers and packaging for medical goods and food would also be treated cardboard. When the tents wear out and the packaging is discarded, though, it shows its true nature—for each panel of cardboard would be impregnated with appropriate local seeds, spores of topsoil fungi and harmless fertilizing agents, so that by tearing them up and watering them, refugees could start gardens, complete with mulch, fertilizer and the microorganisms good soil needs. Even clothing and blankets can be designed to be composted as they wear out.

The entire transitional tent city can end up plowed into gardens as the refugees settle in to stability—and food is not all that can be grown. Fast-growing, salt-absorbing hybrid shade trees can go in as wind-breaks, helping to check erosion and desalinize the soil. If nearby areas have been mined, refugees can also broadcast the seeds for land-mine detecting flowers, local wildflowers which have been smart-bred to change color when they detect nitrogen dioxide in the soil (a chemical leaked by the explosives in the mines as they decay), like those being developed by the Danish Institute of Molecular Biology. More, some have proposed land-mine eating flowers, plants that'd send their roots towards explosives and grow around them, aiding their decomposition and perhaps triggering their explosion. Finally, if the land has been heavily polluted (a frequent consequence of war and civil unrest) specially-bred versions of hearty weed-like native plants which can slurp heavy metals out of the soil, concentrating them for safe disposal, even later reuse, and keeping them out of drinking water.

—but that doesn't mean that we can't do a hell of a lot better than the current reality: grim, sprawling, muddy, overcrowded and septic tent cities where services are rare and opportunities to actually work to improve one's life are few and far between. Tent cities now are often nothing more than places to warehouse people we don't care enough about to much notice. We can do much better.

Beginning with how we build these first, temporary camps, we can think differently about the goal of relief and reconstruction:

"Encouraging communities to be active participants in the rebuilding is key to creating sustainable solutions and to reducing the impact of a disaster. Representatives from the International Red Cross (IRC) spoke at the (last) World Urban Forum on disaster relief and noted the new city of Ciudad Espuma in Honduras—built after Hurricane Mitch swept through in 1998—was the best example of a 'disaster reduction initiative.' The 14,000 families who have lost homes had rebuilt their own houses with an awareness of the potential of future disaster."

Chinese factory workers make compostable tents for distribution to millions of Chinese left homeless by the May 28, 2008, earthquake.

New approaches to working with design for the very poorest can involve the refugees from this disaster in the reconstruction of their own lives. Microlending [the extension of a very small loan to the poor, who otherwise could not qualify for a larger, more traditional loan] programs can be quickly established to provide capital for transitional small businesses, and combined with recovery aid to reunite farmers and fishermen with plows and nets.

Getting Everyone Involved

One of the first steps should be to get the kids learning again. As *Forced Migration Review* (perhaps the most disturbingly-titled social studies publication in the world, if ya' really think about it) says, by creating "safe zones" for kids, and providing access to essential knowledge, educators not only help the whole community return to a sense of psychological stability, but can save a generation which might otherwise be lost. Indeed, by involving elders and parents in the process, a whole community can be moved out of traumatic shock into action.

Meanwhile, technology and collaboration can also help the refugees process the emotional damage and mentally begin rebuilding. Cheap, discardable videocameras could offer them the opportunity to record their stories, in order to begin healing and take an inventory of the skills the refugees bring. Open source textbooks rendered into the local language through collaborative translation can help spread literacy and education quickly through the population. Telecentros and other community technology resources can help bring real opportunity even to impoverished rural people, while, in the bigger picture, helping to redistribute the future.

A primary goal of the first couple years of relief and reconstruction work should be to help arm these communities with the expertise, technology and capital to "leapfrog" over older, out-moded, costly and centralized technologies and start right in on building lives of sustainable prosperity.

This process should start the moment boots hit the ground. Relief is not simply about saving lives (though that is of course the top priority)—relief is also the first step in the reconstruction. In the next months, vast efforts will go into building roads, air strips, water and power systems, emergency clinics and other infrastructure to support relief efforts. With that in mind, big international NGOs [Non-Governmental Organizations] ought to be thinking, whenever possible, about the long-term utility of that infrastructure to the local communities. Can these huge investments be structured in ways that not only save lives today, but improve the community tomorrow?

Solar Energy

An example: many relief efforts should include solar energy, right from the beginning:

"A viable use for PV is to meet the emergency demands in large-scale disasters, where power will be out for long periods of time and survivor support is difficult to provide due to the extensive area destroyed. Massive infrastructure damage makes refueling generators a challenge, as pumping stations are often inoperable and roads impassable. Power distribution lines are difficult to fix because of the impassable roads, much less transporting materials for reconstruction. When a disaster strikes an island and the port is destroyed, shipping fuel for generators becomes a problem. . . . There are inappropriate applications for photovoltaics in response to disasters. The large-scale power needs of sewer and water facilities, hospitals, large shelters, distribution and emergency operations centers are better met with gasoline or diesel generators in an emergency."

But solar panels don't just fill many emergency roles better than generators could. Widespread use of solar energy in the disaster relief efforts will also provide kernels of equipment, infrastructure and expertise around which communities can build distributed energy systems—the kind of systems more likely to work for many developing world communities in the long run. They can become a sort of seed-stock for new developing world smart grids, LEDs, access to computation and communications, village technologies and renewable energy, even better shelter—the "bright lights, small villages" strategy.

Then, as the rebuilding commences in earnest, people can aspire to really move forward. There's no reason why the area which now lies ruined could not be something like a technologically empowered Costa Rica in ten years: prosperous (at least by developing world standards) and green, reasonably stable and well-governed, prepared for future disasters, and choosing its own future.

Copyright 2008 by Mike Keefe, *The Denver Post*, and CagleCartoons.com.

Let's not just "restore to them an equal portion." Instead, let's give them the opportunity to imagine an entirely new future. Let's not stop at saving lives and easing suffering today so they can return tomorrow to poverty in the shadow of an increasingly angry climate. Let's go farther. Let's change the dynamic. Let's help them make themselves into the stories we tell when we want to explain how things can be made better, the examples of how lives can be improved—a better future made real where today there is only misery.

FOURTEEN

Tsunami Survivors Inspired to Help Katrina Victims

Kris Axtman

Kris Axtman is a staff writer for the *Christian Science Monitor*. In this viewpoint Axtman profiles several Indonesian tsunami survivors who decided to volunteer to help victims of Hurricane Katrina. The volunteers were inspired by the support that they received after the 2004 tsunami, when they were in a similar situation. The volunteers were surprised by the welcome they received and planned to take the American sense of volunteerism back to Indonesia. Americans can also learn from the Indonesians about community organizing and other concepts that help victims take the next step in recovery.

Insafi Gulo was asleep above the shop where she worked on the island of Nias when an aftershock rocked the west coast of Indonesia three months after the tsunami.

The five-story building collapsed, trapping her beneath piles of rubble. Worried she wouldn't be found in time, she eventually freed herself, losing her right foot in the process.

After receiving a prosthesis, and more than a year of rehabilitation, Ms. Gulo is now a volunteer here in the United States, ripping out drywall and hammering nails in devastated communities along Mississippi's Gulf Coast. She is one of eight

Kris Axtman, "Returning Favor, Indonesians Aid Katrina's Victims," *The Christian Science Monitor*, April 4, 2006. Reproduced by permission from *The Christian Science Monitor* (www.csmonitor.com).

Indonesian tsunami survivors and aid workers who, having witnessed international relief firsthand, are now reciprocating with some of their own.

And though it's their first trip to America, their first experience with cold weather, and their first time in a thrift shop and

Chinese actor and tsunami survivor Jet Li attended tsunami relief fund-raising concerts in 2005.

a casino, the volunteers have found common ground with those they aid.

"It makes me really happy to help people who suffered the way I did," says Gulo as a smile works its way across her face.

The volunteers' two-week trip was inspired by a letter to aid groups. "I believe that people in New Orleans—victims of Katrina—must have . . . supported victims of Tsunami in Aceh—through many kinds of supports," wrote Sigit Wijayanta, executive director of the Christian Foundation for Community Development in Indonesia. "We are also eager to seek for what kind of help we can offer to the victims of Katrina to release some of their burden."

US Group Funds Trip

Presbyterian Disaster Assistance, which had been working in Indonesia since the 2004 tsunami, responded. It helped pick the volunteers and funded their two-week trip to the US. The volunteers rebuild homes by day, sleep in tents at night, and make friends wherever they go.

"I was nervous about coming because I thought that Americans were mean to everyone," says Triayu Prastiwi Kodrat, a relief worker with Church World Service-Indonesia, who has become partial to Lays potato chips and sweet tea. "But everybody has been so nice and they want us to feel good here."

Besides the change in attitude (even though the Indonesian men were detained by US immigration officials for 2-1/2 hours), Ms. Kodrat says she will bring back to her country the sense of volunteerism that pervades US culture.

In Indonesia, her relief group had to post want ads and pay salaries when it needed help after the tsunami. "But that's not the way it is in America," she says. "People come and volunteer without getting paid."

Novianus Patanduka, also with the Church World Service-Indonesia, left a 3-day-old baby to come to the US. "It really affected our hearts when we saw what happened here. It was the same thing that happened in the tsunami."

Tsunami: December 26, 2004

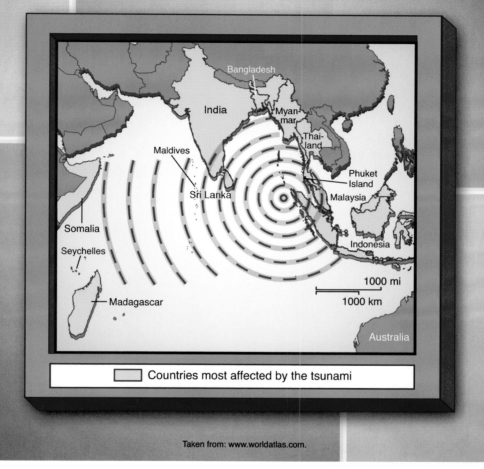

Countries most affected by the tsunami

Taken from: www.worldatlas.com.

Even so, the wealth—even in America's poorest state—surprised him: "You really can't compare the suffering of Katrina with the suffering of the tsunami. Here, even the poorest people still have cars beside their [government- provided] trailers. When you go out into the most devastated parts of Indonesia, all the people have is their own physical strength."

Mr. Novianus also noticed that US progress seven months after the natural disaster was much more rapid than Indonesia's—in part, he believes, because those affected are much more active participants in reconstruction.

Lessons from the Indonesians

While the Indonesians were impressed by America's disaster-response and volunteerism, there are many things Americans can learn from them, says Rebecca Young, liaison for the tsunami-recovery effort of Presbyterian Disaster Assistance.

"They are actually better about community organizing, teaching people how to set up cooperatives, and creating revolving loan programs—all of which creates economic independence," says Ms. Young, also a Presbyterian minister. "I've never been comfortable with America's soup-kitchen kind of response. We give [people in need] stuff but we don't take that next step to help them stand on their own."

One night last week at a Baptist church in Biloxi, Miss., hurricane survivors treated the Indonesians to a dinner of homemade red beans and rice, chicken gumbo, collard greens, and sweet potato pie and told their stories.

Flora Jackson described how she and her family escaped drowning. "After three or four days, I was so hungry. I didn't know what to do," she says. The Indonesians nod with understanding. After dinner, they hug the Katrina survivors and leave them with a song.

"The Lord is my strength," their voices blended in Indonesian. "Even if the earth shakes and the storms come. I'll fly high with him."

What You Should Know About Disaster Relief

What Is Disaster Relief?

Disaster relief is usually defined as procedures to help people directly affected by disasters such as epidemics, earthquakes, floods, and fires. This help may come in the form of rescuing people from danger during and after a disaster, providing food, water, and temporary shelter, and assisting with postdisaster cleanup and rebuilding of affected areas. Humanitarian organizations such as the Federal Emergency Management Agency (FEMA), the United Way, and the Red Cross are often employed in relief efforts.

How a Country Receives Disaster Relief

- Agencies such as the International Federation of Red Cross and Red Crescent Societies (IFRC) can assist disaster relief efforts only if they are specifically asked to do so by an affected country.
- Because of political reasons, some governments choose not to receive foreign aid after a natural disaster. However, this decision not to receive help may be appealed if other countries' governments can prove that the people in an affected area are in dire need of foreign assistance.
- When a country does request aid, this call for assistance must specifically note the kind of relief that is required, and it must pinpoint where the help is needed.

Some Basic Disaster Relief Regulations
- Relief efforts must be responsive to victims with special needs such as women, children, and the elderly.
- Relief must coordinate with an affected country's own relief efforts in progress, and it must strengthen, not hinder them.
- Relief efforts must be carried out in a way that limits the negative impact on the affected country after the relief workers leave.

Rules Relief Workers Must Follow
- Whatever organization they belong to, relief workers must abide by the laws of the country affected by disaster while they are helping there.
- A visa must be given to relief workers by the country in need, so they can enter the country and travel around freely.
- Aid must be given based on need alone and not be motivated by political aspirations.
- No legal, political, or religious standpoint can be addressed to disaster victims by relief workers. Aid must be provided by competent workers who are sensitive to the culture of the victims of the disaster.
- Relief is to be given without regard to race, religion, or class, according to the IFRC's regulations.

Initial Relief in a Disaster
- The population of an affected area that is most threatened by disastrous conditions must be evacuated quickly and carefully.
- Evacuation efforts should include rescuing people trapped or stranded by the disaster.
- On-the-spot first aid should be administered to injured people if possible, but if they require more than basic first aid they should be referred to capable medical facilities nearby.
- Evacuation efforts should also include temporary shelters for those suddenly made homeless by a disaster.
- Emergency food and water must be given to all people who need it.

- Immediate psychological help must be given to the disaster survivors who require such attention.

Disaster Relief Acts in the United States

- The Disaster Relief Act of 1974 (Public Law 93-288) is the federal law in the United States that first established the president's power to make disaster declarations after natural disasters and other catastrophic emergencies. In 1979 President Jimmy Carter consolidated many of the more than one hundred federal agencies in charge of disaster relief into the Federal Emergency Management Agency (FEMA).
- In November 1988 the United States Congress amended the Disaster Relief Act and renamed it the Stafford Disaster Relief and Emergency Assistance Act (Public Law 100-707). The various amendments strove to make disaster relief response in the United States more orderly and systematic for state and local governments during times of crisis. In particular, the new act grants FEMA the responsibility for coordinating both financial and physical relief efforts during disaster and for implementing contributions by other relief agencies. The amended act is named for Republican senator and former governor of Vermont Robert Stafford, who was instrumental in lobbying for the passage of the law.
- Pets Evacuation and Transportation Standards Act (Public Law 109-308) amended the Stafford Act when President George W. Bush signed the act into law in October 2006. In the wake of Hurricane Katrina in 2005, tens of thousands of pets perished or were left homeless after being separated from their owners during the disaster. Relief workers did not allow pets to accompany citizens as they were forced to evacuate the affected Gulf Coast regions. The new law now requires states seeking FEMA assistance to allow for the accommodation of pets and service animals during evacuations.

Disaster Relief in the United States

- In 2008 the Federal Emergency Management Agency responded to seventy-five disaster declarations in the United States.

- Hurricane Katrina claimed the lives of over 1,800 people and caused more than $84 billion in damage in 2005. Also in 2005, Hurricane Rita killed 120 people and caused $10 billion in damage. Hurricane Gustav killed at least 153 people in 2008 and caused more than $8 billion in damage. Hurricane Ike also claimed 112 lives in the United States in 2008 and left behind $24 billion in damages.
- Since Hurricane Katrina, the Salvation Army has raised over $365 million for various U.S. disaster relief efforts.
- In 2008 the U.S. government sent $4.9 million in aid to support earthquake victims in China's Sichuan Province. The quake killed more than sixty-nine thousand people.
- In 2008 the U.S. government also sent more than $47 million to victims of Cyclone Nargis in Myanmar.
- In 2008 the American Red Cross reported that it expected to spend in excess of $15 million on disaster relief within the year, for both recent and future disasters.

What You Should Do About Disaster Relief

Natural disasters affect millions of people worldwide every year. According to the International Strategy for Disaster Reduction organization, in 2004 alone nearly 400,000 people were reportedly killed or directly affected by some form of natural disaster. With the United States ranking third in the world for most frequently occurring disasters, safety precautions should be well planned in case of such emergencies.

Helping Your Family Prepare for a Disaster

Knowing how to best prepare for an event and knowing what to expect can significantly reduce the stress and confusion that can arise when dealing with a natural disaster. If your parents do not have a disaster preparedness plan for your family, you might take the time now to work on one together.

The best place to begin when thinking about disaster preparation is in your own neighborhood. Basic preparations are sometimes the most important. For instance, having an evacuation route mapped out and a safe house or shelter already in mind will allow you and your family to respond more quickly to official evacuation orders, should they occur. If you are evacuated from your home because of a disaster, it is also smart to have an emergency kit ready to go. Encourage your family to create a well-stocked emergency kit consisting of water and food to last at least three days, blankets and clothing, first-aid supplies and a stock of personal medications, flashlights and batteries, a telephone, emergency cash, copies of important documents such as insurance papers and Social Security cards, and a contact list for emergency services.

Preparing for a Disaster at School

In all likelihood, your school is already well prepared to handle the kinds of natural disasters that are most likely to affect your area. If you are unsure about your school's preparedness, it is a good idea to check with a teacher or administrator. At the very least, the students at your school should know which disasters could occur in your area and how to prepare for each disaster at school. Students should learn how they would be warned of an emergency, and they should also know both the campus's and your community's evacuation routes. Students with disabilities and other special needs should also learn what special arrangements have been made for their safety, should a disaster strike during school hours.

Get Involved in Disaster Relief

If you live in an area that is not affected by a recent catastrophic disaster, you may choose to help others in need elsewhere. You can organize your school, church, or other youth group to hold a fund-raiser for disaster victims. Cash donations or donations of food, clothing, or cleaning supplies can be sent to the victims of natural disasters through one of any number of disaster relief agencies. Just be sure to check with relief organizations first, to ensure that the goods and services you have to offer are immediately needed in the affected disaster area.

Should a disaster happen nearby, you may even have an opportunity to go on location as a volunteer to help with the cleanup and rebuilding efforts. Some organizations are specifically looking for young adult volunteers. The National Relief Network, for instance, is just one of many groups that recruits volunteer groups of thirty-five members each, ages thirteen and up, to help aid in community rebuilding when a natural disaster is declared. This organization is approved by the National Honor Society and the National Association of Student Councils.

Finally, you do not have to wait until a disaster strikes to seek out opportunities to help others; organizations such as the Red Cross are in need of support year-round so that they may be prepared for unexpected and catastrophic disasters. Creating emergency kits that can be used in the event of an emergency is just one example of activities that can be ongoing and will be critical when a disaster strikes.

ORGANIZATIONS TO CONTACT

The editors have compiled the following list of organizations concerned with the issues debated in this book. The descriptions are derived from materials provided by the organizations. All have publications or information available for interested readers. The list was compiled on the date of publication of the present volume; the information provided here may change. Be aware that many organizations take several weeks or longer to respond to inquiries, so allow as much time as possible.

American Red Cross
2025 E St. NW
Washington, DC 20006
(703) 206-6000
Web site: www.redcross.org

Founded in 1881 by Clara Barton, the American Red Cross is the nation's premier emergency response organization. The American Red Cross places emphasis on six areas through which they can assist communities: educational programs promoting health and safety, community services that help the needy, the collection and distribution of blood and blood products, international relief and development programs, support for military families, and domestic disaster relief. Each year, the American Red Cross responds to more than seventy thousand disasters, focusing on immediate emergency needs such as food, shelter, physical health services, and mental health services.

Center for International Disaster Information (CIDI)
4100 N. Fairfax Dr.
Arlington, VA 22203
(703) 243-8900
e-mail: rmuffley@cidi.org
Web site: www.cidi.org

The CIDI was established in 1988 to handle the growing number of donations to disaster relief made by individuals and businesses. The CIDI provides relevant articles on disasters and disaster relief, current and historical reports of countries affected by disasters, and news to better educate those who wish to donate money and want to make sure that their contribution is being used in a productive way.

Federal Emergency Management Agency (FEMA)
500 C St. SW
Washington, DC 20472
(800) 621-3362
e-mail: FEMA-Correspondence-Unit@dhs.gov
Web site: www.fema.gov

The primary mission of FEMA is to reduce the loss of life and property and protect the nation from all hazards, including natural disasters, acts of terrorism, and other man-made disasters. FEMA is responsible for managing disaster relief efforts in the United States by developing plans of preparedness, protection, response, and recovery. The FEMA Web site features a list of recent disasters and emergencies, FEMA's current activities, as well as a list of programs and services available to communities experiencing an emergency. In March 2003 FEMA became a part of the Department of Homeland Security.

National Drought Mitigation Center (NDMC)
University of Nebraska–Lincoln
819 Hardin Hall
3310 Holdrege St.
PO Box 830988
Lincoln, NE 68583-0988
(402) 472-6707
e-mail: ndmc@unl.edu
Web site: www.drought.unl.edu

The NDMC, based at the University of Nebraska at Lincoln, provides information about drought and drought prevention and helps people and institutions develop and institute measures to reduce societal vulnerability to drought. The NDMC stresses preparation and risk management.

United Nations Center for Regional Development (UNCRD)
Disaster Management Planning Hyogo Office
Hito-Mirai Kan 5th Floor
1-5-2 Wakihama-kaigan-dori, Chuo-ku
Kobe, Japan 651-0073
81-78-262-5560
e-mail: rep@hyogo.uncrd.or.jp
Web site: www.hyogo.uncrd.or.jp

The UNCRD Hyogo Office was established in 1999 in Kobe, Japan, to provide advisory services to communities vulnerable to disasters. In cooperation with governmental agencies, nongovernmental agencies (NGOs), and academic institutions, UNCRD aims to improve the safety of core community facilities such as schools and hospitals, houses, and cultural heritage sites that are vulnerable to disasters. UNCRD also offers recovery assistance for countries stricken by large-scale disasters.

United Nations International Strategy for Disaster Reduction (ISDR)
International Environment House II
7-9 Chemin de Balexert
CH 1219 Chatelaine
Geneva 10, Switzerland
41-22-917-8908 or 8907
e-mail: isdr@un.org
Web site: www.unisdr.org

The ISDR's mission is to build disaster-resilient communities by promoting the importance of disaster reduction during the design and construction of these communities. The ISDR aims to reduce human, economic, and environmental losses due to disasters. The organization also aims to increase public awareness of risk and vulnerability and to increase scientific knowledge about disaster reduction.

United Nations Relief Web
Relief Web New York
Office for the Coordination of Humanitarian Affairs
United Nations
New York, NY 10017
(212) 963-1234
Web site: www.reliefweb.int/rw/dbc.nsf/doc100?OpenForm

Relief Web was launched by the United Nations Office for the Coordination of Humanitarian Affairs in October of 1996. Relief Web is the world's leading Web site for documents and maps relating to humanitarian emergencies and disasters and was specifically designed to assist the international humanitarian community in the effective delivery of emergency assistance.

United States Agency for International Development (USAID)
Ronald Reagan Building
Washington, DC 20523-1000
(202) 712-0000
e-mail: pinquiries@usaid.gov
Web site: www.usaid.gov

USAID is an independent federal government agency that receives foreign policy guidance from the secretary of state. The USAID was created in 1961 to provide foreign assistance to countries in need. The USAID supports long-term and equitable economic growth and advances U.S. foreign policy objectives by also supporting agriculture and trade, global health, democracy, conflict prevention, and humanitarian assistance.

BIBLIOGRAPHY

Books

Bob Arnot and Mark Cohen, *Your Survival: The Complete Resource for Disaster Planning and Recovery*. Long Island City, NY: Hatherleigh, October 2007.

Mike Bryan and Ivor Van Heerden, *The Storm: What Went Wrong and Why During Hurricane Katrina—The Inside Story from One Louisiana Scientist*. New York: Penguin, 2006.

David Bentley Hart, *The Doors of the Sea: Where Was God in the Tsunami?* Grand Rapids, MI: Eerdmans, 2005.

Chester Hartman and Gregory D. Squires, *There Is No Such Thing as a Natural Disaster: Race, Class, and Hurricane Katrina*. New York: Taylor & Francis, 2006.

Jed Horne, *Breach of Faith: Hurricane Katrina and the Near Death of a Great American City*. New York: Random House, 2008.

Roger G. Kennedy, *Wildfire and Americans: How to Save Lives, Property, and Your Tax Dollars*. New York: Farrar, Straus and Giroux, 2006.

H. Michael Mogil, *Extreme Weather: Understanding the Science of Hurricanes, Tornadoes, Floods, Heat Waves, Snow Storms, Global Warming, and Other Atmospheric Disturbances*. New York: Black Dog & Leventhal, 2007.

Cal Orey, *The Man Who Predicts Earthquakes: Jim Berkland, Maverick Geologist: How His Quake Warnings Can Save Lives*. Boulder, CO: Sentient Publications, 2006.

Amanda Ripley, *The Unthinkable: Who Survives When Disaster Strikes—and Why*. New York: Random House, 2008.

Cathy Scott, *Pawprints of Katrina: Pets Saved and Lessons Learned*. Hoboken, NJ: Wiley, John & Sons, 2008.

Periodicals

Marilyn Blake, "Tornadoes—Not Just in Kansas," *Rural Telecommunications*, July 1, 2007.

Elisabeth Boone, "Tsunami!" *Rough Notes*, May 1, 2005.

Bryan Brown, "After Katrina: Three Years After One of the Country's Worst Natural Disasters, New Orleans Is Still Struggling to Rebuild," *Junior Scholastic*, September 1, 2008.

Current Events, "California Firestorm: 'Devil Winds' Whip Up Wildfires from Malibu to Mexico," November 5, 2007.

Aaron Derr, "Lending a Hand: Make Sure Your Troop Is Prepared to Help After an Emergency," *Boys' Life*, January 2006.

Marcus Grant, "What Are Hurricanes?" *News, Opinion, and Commentary Community*, December 13, 2007.

Audrey Hudson, "Gustav Slams Better Prepared Gulf," *Washington Times*, September 2, 2008.

Robert C. Morrow and D. Mark Llewellyn, "Tsunami Overview," *Military Medicine*, October 1, 2006.

Sid Perkins, "Storm Center: A Detailed Look Inside the Core of a Hurricane," *Science News*, June 23, 2007.

John C. Pine, "Hurricane Katrina and Oil Spills: Impact on Coastal and Ocean Environments," *Oceanography*, vol. 19, no. 2, June 2006.

Glen B. Stewart, "Hurricane Season Preparation Tips for 2008—a Short List of Must Haves and a Few Life-Saving Gems," *Family and Marriage Community*, June 16, 2008.

Michael Stone, "How Not to Respond to a Crisis," *New Statesman*, January 9, 2006.

Alison Thorne, "Exploiting Tragedy: How Tsunami Relief Aid Is Used in Economic and Military Power Plays," *Freedom-Socialist*, April/May 2005.

Frank Vanderlugt, "Katrina Most Expensive U.S. Disaster," *News, Opinion, and Commentary Community*, December 13, 2007.

Gary A. Warner, "Along the Edge: Traveling the San Andreas Fault," *Orange County Register*, April 16, 2006.

INDEX

PICTURE CREDITS